Report to the Ranking Member,
Subcommittee on Immigration,
Refugees and Border Security,
Committee on the Judiciary,
U.S. Senate

July 2013

U.S.-MEXICO BORDER

I0448300

CBP Action Needed to Improve Wait Time Data and Measure Outcomes of Trade Facilitation Efforts

July 2013

U.S.-MEXICO BORDER

CBP Action Needed to Improve Wait Time Data and Measure Outcomes of Trade Facilitation Efforts

GAO Highlights

Highlights of GAO-13-603, a report to Ranking Member, Subcommittee on Immigration, Refugees and Border Security, Committee on the Judiciary, U.S. Senate.

Why GAO Did This Study

Trade with Mexico is important to the United States' economy. Most of this trade crosses the border by truck, and studies have shown that long waits at border crossings can negatively affect the U.S. economy. CBP is responsible for securing U.S. borders at ports of entry to prevent illegal entry of persons and contraband while also facilitating legitimate trade and travel. GAO was asked to examine CBP data on and actions taken to address wait times at southwest border crossings. This report addresses the extent to which (1) CBP wait time data are reliable for public reporting and informing CBP decisions, (2) CBP has identified infrastructure and staffing needed to process current commercial traffic volumes, and (3) CBP performance measures assess progress toward its trade facilitation goal. GAO assessed the reliability of CBP's wait time data; visited six land border crossings (not generalizable, but selected largely for high traffic volume); analyzed CBP documentation, including needs assessments; and interviewed stakeholders and CBP officials.

What GAO Recommends

GAO recommends that CBP (1) determine and take steps to help ensure consistent implementation of existing wait time data collection methodologies, (2) assess the feasibility of replacing current methodologies with automated methods, (3) document its staff allocation process and rationale, and (4) develop outcome-oriented performance measures. DHS agreed with these four recommendations and identified steps to address them, although the planned actions will not address the intent of one.

View GAO-13-603. For more information, contact Rebecca Gambler at (202) 512-8777 or gamblerr@gao.gov.

What GAO Found

Within the Department of Homeland Security (DHS), U.S. Customs and Border Protection's (CBP) data on commercial vehicle wait times—the time it takes to travel from the end of the queue to the CBP primary inspection point at land border crossings—are unreliable for public reporting and CBP management decisions across border crossings. These data—which are collected manually by CBP officers—are unreliable because CBP officers inconsistently implement an approved data collection methodology, and the methodologies used vary by crossing. For example, five of the six crossings GAO visited require observation of the end of the queue to estimate wait times, but officials at these crossings reported the lines extended beyond their view at times. As a result, these data are generally not used by the private sector and are of limited usefulness for CBP management decisions on staffing and infrastructure investments. Determining and taking steps to help CBP officials overcome challenges to consistent implementation of existing methodologies could improve the reliability and usefulness of CBP's current wait time data. CBP officials have identified automated wait time data collection technology as the best way to improve data reliability. The Department of Transportation (DOT), in coordination with state DOTs and CBP, has ongoing pilot projects to use technology to gather more reliable wait time data at some border crossings. However, CBP has not assessed the feasibility of replacing current methods with automated data collection. Doing so, consistent with program management standards, could help CBP determine how to best improve data reliability.

CBP officials report and analyses indicate infrastructure and staff needs, but documenting CBP's staff allocation process could improve transparency and facilitate review and validation by CBP and others. CBP officials and analyses identify needs for additional infrastructure—such as more lanes—at some crossings, and GAO analysis of CBP data on lane use generally supported agency views on the extent to which CBP opens lanes at the six crossings GAO visited. Further, GAO analysis of lane use and traffic volume data generally supported CBP officials' statements that they open and close primary inspection lanes in response to fluctuations in commercial traffic volume. CBP analyses identified a need for 3,811 additional officers, and CBP headquarters officials told GAO all southwest border ports require additional staff, but CBP field and port managers at three of six crossings GAO visited reported having sufficient staff. CBP human capital officials reported that they adjust staff allocations across locations to better ensure that staff levels match areas of greatest need, but CBP has not documented this process, and there is no guidance defining the methodology used or factors considered when allocating staff across ports. Documenting this process, consistent with internal control standards, could improve transparency, helping CBP and others to better ensure that scarce staff resources are effectively allocated to fulfill mission needs across ports.

CBP does not have outcome-oriented performance measures to determine the extent to which the agency is facilitating trade. The Office of Management and Budget and GAO guidance recommend using outcome-oriented measures to promote accountability for results. In the absence of such measures, it is difficult for the agency or others to gauge CBP's progress in meeting its stated goal of facilitating trade.

_____ United States Government Accountability Office

Contents

Tables

Figures

Abbreviations

ARRA	American Recovery and Reinvestment Act
ATU	Advance Targeting Unit
CBP	U.S. Customs and Border Protection
CIP	capital investment plan
C-TPAT	Customs and Trade Partnership Against Terrorism
DHS	Department of Homeland Security
DOT	Department of Transportation
FAST	Free and Secure Trade
FDA	Food and Drug Administration
FHWA	Federal Highway Administration
FOUO	for official use only
GDP	gross domestic product
GPRA	Government Performance and Results Act
GSA	General Services Administration
OA	Office of Administration
OFO	Office of Field Operations
OMB	Office of Management and Budget
SRA	Strategic Resource Assessment
WHTI	Western Hemisphere Travel Initiative

GAO U.S. GOVERNMENT ACCOUNTABILITY OFFICE

441 G St. N.W.
Washington, DC 20548

July 24, 2013

The Honorable John Cornyn
Ranking Member
Subcommittee on Immigration, Refugees
    and Border Security
Committee on the Judiciary
United States Senate

Dear Senator Cornyn:

Trade with Mexico, the nation's third-largest trade partner behind Canada and China, is important to the United States' economic health, and timely access to Mexican goods is important to both U.S. manufacturers and consumers. The value of goods imported into the United States from Mexico has increased over 30 percent in the last 5 years, and in 2012 imports from Mexico were valued at nearly $278 billion. Most of this trade crosses the border by commercial truck, and in 2012 there were over 5 million truck crossings into the United States from Mexico. Industry representatives who rely on commercial vehicles to quickly transport goods across the U.S.-Mexico border have raised concerns about long waits at border crossings, and several studies have shown that the time that commercial vehicles spend waiting to cross into the United States from Mexico can have a negative impact on the U.S. economy in terms of lost revenue and jobs.

The Department of Homeland Security's (DHS) U.S. Customs and Border Protection (CBP) is the lead federal agency charged with a dual mission of keeping terrorists, criminals, and inadmissible aliens out of the country while facilitating the flow of legitimate travel and commerce at the nation's borders.[1] CBP's Office of Field Operations (OFO) is responsible for cargo and passenger processing activities related to security, trade,

---

[1]The agency's trade facilitation goals are articulated in DHS's February 2010 *Quadrennial Homeland Security Review Report,* which outlined a strategic framework for homeland security. The two relevant mission goals are to (1) prevent the illegal flow of people and goods across U.S. air, land, and sea borders while expediting the safe flow of lawful travel and commerce, and (2) ensure security and resilience of global movement systems (which includes global trading and transportation networks). See DHS, *Quadrennial Homeland Security Review Report: A Strategic Framework for a Secure Homeland* (Washington, D.C.: February 2010).

immigration, and agricultural inspection at air, land, and sea ports of entry, and CBP's Office of Administration (OA) is responsible for real estate management, including the construction, maintenance, and leasing of facilities, such as land ports of entry.[2] CBP's focus has historically been on security; however, CBP has also undertaken specific efforts to facilitate legitimate travel and trade, such as launching the Free and Secure Trade (FAST) program in 2002 to expedite the travel of low-risk screened shipments across the border, and publishing border crossing wait times on a website to inform public and private sector border crossing decisions.

We previously reported that CBP has faced challenges balancing the goals of security and trade facilitation, and some information necessary to assess its trade facilitation efforts has not been available.[3] Specifically, we reported in July 2010 that CBP's Automated Commercial Environment collected data on freight processing but did not differentiate between FAST and non-FAST shipments—information needed to help CBP determine the extent to which FAST program participants experience intended benefits.[4] We recommended that CBP (1) develop milestones for completing enhancement of the database used to capture data on FAST program benefits, and (2) conduct a study to determine if program benefits are being realized that could help CBP determine what program adjustments, if any, are needed. CBP agreed with these recommendations; took action to collect the needed data; and, as of June 2013, drafted an evaluation of FAST lanes and commercial traffic at select crossings on the northern border to determine whether there is a need to expand the usage of FAST lanes. This study is currently under

---

[2]The General Services Administration (GSA) also has responsibilities related to the construction and maintenance of GSA-owned facilities that include land ports of entry. Ports of entry are the facilities that provide for the controlled entry into or departure from the United States for persons and materials. Specifically, a port of entry is any officially designated location (seaport, airport, or land border location) where DHS officers or employees are assigned to clear passengers and merchandise, collect duties, and enforce customs laws. A single land port of entry may be composed of one or more crossings. For example, the Port of Laredo, Texas, headed by a port director, oversees operations at four separate border crossings, one rail crossing, and one airport. CBP operates 168 land border crossings, 46 of which are located on the southwest border.

[3]GAO, *Border Security: CBP Lacks the Data Needed to Assess the FAST Program at U.S. Northern Border Ports*, GAO-10-694 (Washington, D.C.: July 19, 2010).

[4]CBP's Automated Commercial Environment is CBP's commercial trade processing system—one of several databases and tools used by CBP to screen and assign risk levels to travelers and cargo entering the United States.

review and CBP expects to fully implement this recommendation by December 30, 2013.

You asked us to review what data CBP collects and reports on wait times for commercial vehicles at southwest border land ports of entry and actions CBP has taken to reduce those wait times. This report addresses the following questions:

- To what extent are CBP wait time data reliable for public reporting and informing CBP decisions on staffing and infrastructure investments?

- To what extent has CBP identified infrastructure and staffing needed to process current commercial traffic volume at select southwest border crossings with high traffic volume?

- To what extent do CBP performance measures assess progress toward its goal of facilitating trade?

This report also presents information on the results of studies that have quantified the economic impact of commercial vehicle wait times on cross border commerce. This information, including the methodology used to identify these studies, is presented in appendix I.

To inform our analysis of the first and second objectives, we visited six border crossings—Bridge of the Americas and Ysleta in El Paso, Texas; World Trade Bridge and Columbia Solidarity Bridge in Laredo, Texas; Mariposa in Nogales, Arizona; and Otay Mesa near San Diego, California—selected based on their commercial traffic volume, geographic diversity, and representation of a mix of recent or ongoing infrastructure modernization projects. At each location, we interviewed CBP management, toured the facility, and convened a roundtable of local industry representatives and local government officials. To obtain a range of perspectives on commercial vehicle traffic at southwest border crossings, we met with representatives of 21 companies and associations (who were identified to us as knowledgeable stakeholders representing industries that rely on cross-border commerce, including customs brokers, trucking companies, and distributors) as well as bridge directors and representatives of four local government entities (the Mayors of El Paso and San Diego, the Laredo City Manager, and representatives of the San Diego Association of Governments) at all four cities we visited or by teleconference.[5] We also interviewed officials from federal agencies involved in securing the border and facilitating trade at land ports of entry. Although the results of our site visits and interviews are not generalizable, they provided us with perspectives on operations at ports of entry that accounted for a total of approximately 70 percent of the commercial vehicle crossings into the United States from Mexico for fiscal year 2008 through July 2012. Over the course of our work, we also interviewed other stakeholders, including officials from the Mexican Foreign Ministry, academics, and representatives of national trade associations, such as the American Trucking Associations and the Border Trade Alliance, to obtain a broader range of perspectives on commercial vehicle traffic at southwest border crossings.[6]

To address the first objective, we reviewed and analyzed CBP's policies and guidance for calculating and reporting wait times and CBP evaluations of its wait time data, including a fiscal year 2008 CBP *Commercial Wait Times Analysis Report* completed by CBP's Western Hemisphere Travel Initiative (WHTI) Office.[7] We also reviewed CBP's fiscal year 2012 wait time data for the six crossings we visited and compared documentary and testimonial evidence of how wait times are currently being calculated by officials at land ports of entry on the southwest border against CBP policies and guidance to identify any discrepancies. We also compared CBP's policies and guidance with

---

[5]The San Diego Association of Governments is a public planning, transportation, transit construction, and research agency.

[6]These organizations and officials were identified to us as knowledgeable stakeholders who could provide us with a range of perspectives on commercial vehicle traffic at southwest border crossings. The American Trucking Associations is a national trade and safety organization representing the U.S. trucking industry. The Border Trade Alliance is a nonprofit organization that serves as a forum for participants to address key issues affecting trade, travel, and security in North America.

[7]CBP reported on the reliability of wait time calculations in its *Western Hemisphere Travel Initiative, Commercial Wait Times Analysis Final Report, October 2007-September 2008.* The goal of WHTI is to facilitate entry for U.S. citizens and legitimate foreign visitors while strengthening U.S. border security. The WHTI Program Office sponsored this evaluation of commercial vehicle wait times to validate the current wait time reporting systems at individual crossings and to determine if a national standard for reporting wait times can be established.

criteria in *Standards for Internal Control in the Federal Government*.[8] Our assessment of the reliability of these data is discussed later in this report. To determine the status of the Department of Transportation's (DOT) pilot projects to automate wait time data at the southwest border, we interviewed officials at DOT's Federal Highway Administration (FHWA), Texas Department of Transportation, and Texas A&M University and reviewed documentary evidence they provided, such as written updates on the status of certain pilot projects.[9] We compared CBP's plans to automate wait times with standards for program management.[10]

To address the second objective, we reviewed and analyzed CBP and General Services Administration (GSA) assessments of land port of entry capacity, such as CBP's Strategic Resource Assessments (SRA), and reviewed documentation of CBP's Workload Staffing Model, used to determine staff needs at land ports of entry.[11] We also interviewed CBP and GSA officials about infrastructure needs at land border crossings and how these needs are identified and prioritized. We interviewed CBP officials about the agency's staff allocation policies and processes and compared these with criteria in our previous work on human capital management and *Standards for Internal Control in the Federal*

---

[8]GAO, *Standards for Internal Control in the Federal Government*, GAO/AIMD-00-21.3.1 (Washington, D.C.: November 1999). These standards, issued pursuant to the requirements of the Federal Managers' Financial Integrity Act of 1982, Pub. L. No. 97-255, 96 Stat. 814, provide the overall framework for establishing and maintaining internal control in the federal government.

[9]As described later in this report, automation of wait time data collection relies on Radio-Frequency Identification readers to read the unique signals from passing vehicles at several points along the border-crossing route. These data points are then automatically matched and analyzed to estimate the current wait time at that crossing.

[10]Project Management Institute, *The Standard for Program Management©*, Second Edition, (Newton Square, Pennsylvania: 2008).

[11]The SRA is a needs assessment process by which CBP collects and analyzes information about the infrastructure at each crossing along the northern and southwestern borders, identifies needs, and prioritizes infrastructure improvement projects. CBP officials reported conducting these assessments fiscal years 2003 through 2006.

Government.[12] We also analyzed CBP data on traffic volume and the number of primary lanes open during operating hours at the six crossings from fiscal years 2008 through 2012. We selected this time period for our data analyses to permit a trend analysis. Our data analyses are not generalizable to the entire southwest border, but represent trends at six high-volume crossings. To assess the reliability of these data sources, we reviewed documentation, interviewed agency officials, electronically tested the data, reviewed internal controls, and traced a selection of data to source files. We determined that the data were sufficiently reliable for the purposes of our report.

To address the third objective, we reviewed documentation of CBP's fiscal year 2013 performance goals, measures, and reports. We assessed CBP's measures against criteria in Office of Management and Budget (OMB) Circular No. A-11 and useful practices GAO previously identified to enhance performance management and measurement processes.[13] We also interviewed relevant DHS and CBP officials regarding CBP's current performance measures and the extent to which CBP uses its wait time data to measure progress, among other things.

We also identified studies that quantified the economic impact of commercial vehicle wait times on cross-border commerce by searching literature and asking relevant interviewees whether they were aware of any such studies. We reviewed over 100 identified studies and analyzed the 6 studies that determined an economic impact of commercial vehicle

---

[12]See GAO, *A Model of Strategic Human Capital Management,* GAO-02-373SP (Washington, D.C.: March 2002), and GAO/AIMD-00-21.3.1. The first report descr bes a human capital model we developed that identifies eight critical success factors for managing human capital strategically. In developing this model, we built upon GAO's *Human Capital: A Self-Assessment Checklist for Agency Leaders,* GAO/OCG-00-14G (Washington, D.C.: September 2000). Among other steps, we also considered lessons learned from GAO reports on public and private organizations that are viewed as leaders in strategic human capital management and managing for results.

[13]See OMB Circular No. A-11, *Preparation, Submission, and Execution of the Budget* (Washington, D.C.: Aug. 3, 2012). See also GAO, *Managing for Results: Strengthening Regulatory Agencies' Performance Management Practices,* GAO/GGD-00-10 (Washington, D.C.: Oct. 28, 1999). In this report we gathered information from 23 federal and state organizations that we or other credible sources identified as using or planning to use a variety of useful practices to enhance specific aspects of their performance management and measurement processes. The organizations, although they had different missions, sizes, and organizational structures, said they consistently recognized that these practices are important in their efforts to develop a stronger results orientation.

wait times on the southwest border. A more detailed description of our methodology and the results of these studies are presented in appendix I.

We conducted this performance audit from July 2012 to July 2013 in accordance with generally accepted government auditing standards. Those standards require that we plan and perform the audit to obtain sufficient, appropriate evidence to provide a reasonable basis for our findings and conclusions based on our audit objectives. We believe that the evidence obtained provides a reasonable basis for our findings and conclusions based on our audit objectives. Additional details on our scope and methodology are contained in appendix II.

Background

Agencies' Responsibilities at Land Ports of Entry

In addition to CBP, various agencies have responsibilities for facilitating trade at land ports of entry and conducting inspections of commercial vehicles. GSA oversees design, construction, and maintenance for all ports of entry in consultation with CBP. In consultation with GSA, CBP develops an investment plan to manage the modernization of the land ports of entry inventory. Within DOT, FHWA provides funding for highway and road construction. In addition, the Federal Motor Carrier Safety Administration and state DOTs in some states—Arizona, Texas, and California on the southwest border—may conduct commercial vehicle inspections at or adjacent to land ports of entry to ensure compliance with federal and state-specific safety standards.

In executing its mission, CBP operates 168 land border crossings, which vary in size, location, and commercial traffic volume. Of these, 46 crossings are located on the southwest border, and 24 of these crossings process commercial vehicle traffic. The four largest land border ports of entry on the southwest border by commercial vehicle traffic volume are Laredo, Texas; Otay Mesa, California; El Paso, Texas; and Calexico East, California. See figure 1 for a picture of commercial vehicles in line to enter the United States at the Otay Mesa border crossing near San Diego, California.

Figure 1: Commercial Vehicles in Line to Enter the United States at Otay Mesa near San Diego, California

Source: CBP.

Note: This photo was taken on April 22, 2011.

Inspections of Commercial Vehicles at Land Ports of Entry

Processing commercial vehicles into the United States at land ports of entry involves various steps and requirements.[14] First, CBP requires carriers to submit electronic lists describing their shipments, known as e-Manifests, prior to a shipment's arrival at the border.[15] Second, CBP reviews the e-Manifest using its Automated Commercial Environment

---

[14]For the purpose of this report, we focused on commercial vehicle traffic, as opposed to private vehicle or pedestrian traffic.

[15]The entry document (e-Manifest) contains information about a shipment, including the shipment type, conveyance, passenger/crew, and equipment. E-Manifests for FAST shipments must be submitted 30 minutes before arrival, and e-Manifests for non-FAST shipments must be submitted at least 1 hour before arrival. See 19 C.F.R. § 123.92(a).

database, among others, and assigns a risk level to the shipment.[16] Next, the commercial vehicle proceeds into the United States and to a primary inspection booth at the U.S. port of entry, where a CBP officer reviews documentation on the exporter, importer, and goods being transported. If the documentation is consistent with CBP requirements and no further inspections are required, the truck is allowed to pass through the port. Depending on the port of entry, goods imported, or law enforcement requirements, CBP may direct the commercial truck to secondary inspection. According to CBP, trucks are referred to secondary inspection for numerous reasons, such as officer's initiative, targeted inspection, or random inspection.[17] Secondary inspection involves more detailed document processing and examinations using other methods including gamma ray imaging systems and advanced radiation portal monitors or unloading and physical inspection.[18] Trucks that require secondary inspection may be inspected by more than one federal agency, depending on their cargo.[19] See figure 2 for an illustration of the steps in the commercial vehicle inspection process at land ports of entry.

---

[16]CBP uses various databases and tools, including the Automated Targeting System, Automated Commercial Environment, and local Advance Targeting Units (ATU) to screen and assign risk levels to travelers and cargo entering the United States.

[17]According to CBP, officers select shipments for targeted inspection based on several factors. Specifically, shipments may be selected for targeted inspection based on information provided by the ATUs, Manifest Review Units, Document Analysis Units, and other specialized enforcement units. The ATUs use information from the Automated Targeting System or Automated Commercial Environment to review manifest data prior to the shipments crossing into the United States. The Manifest Review Units are responsible for analyzing manifests, which list in detail the total cargo of shipments. Examples of data elements on a manifest include shipper, point and country of origin of goods, export carrier, and description of packages and goods. The Document Analysis Units are responsble for analyzing fraudulent documents.

[18]Prior to the primary inspection booths, CBP also screens commercial traffic using radiation portal monitors to detect nuclear and radiological materials. Radiation portals are capable of detecting various types of radiation emanating from nuclear devices, dirty bombs, special nuclear materials, natural sources, and isotopes commonly used in medicine and industry. Unlike gamma ray imaging systems—such as CBP's Vehicle and Cargo Inspection System—these devices do not produce images, but are passive systems that alert when energy emitted by radioactive sources is detected.

[19]For example, according to officials with the U.S. Department of Health and Human Services' Food and Drug Administration (FDA), FDA personnel conduct public health inspections on incoming commercial vehicles on the southwest border in an effort to ensure that food and food products from abroad meet U.S. standards.

Figure 2: Commercial Vehicle Inspection Process at a Land Port of Entry

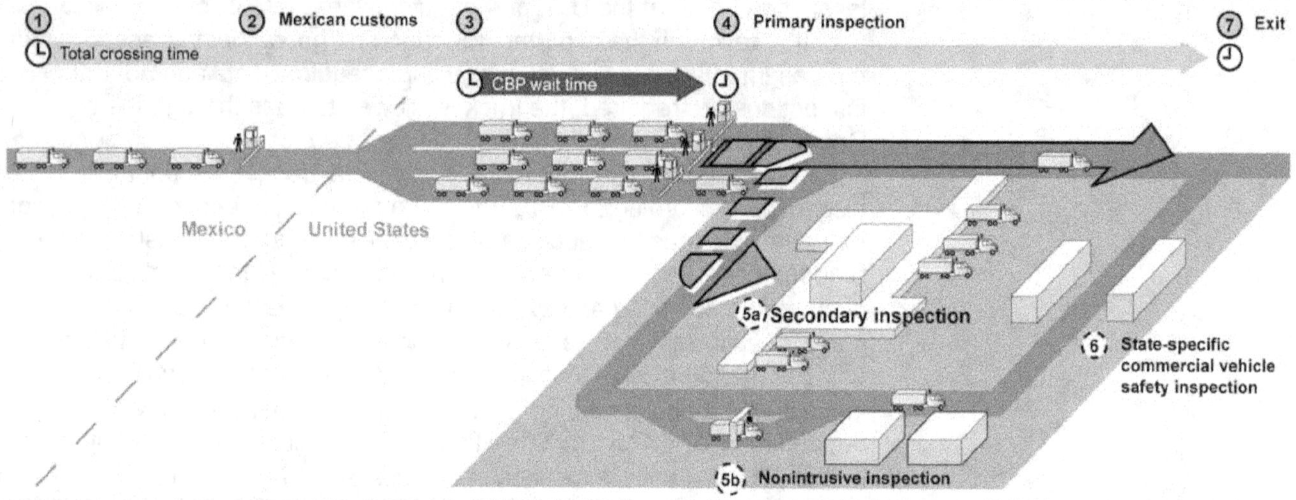

① ② Mexican customs ③ ④ Primary inspection ⑦ Exit

🕐 Total crossing time

🕐 CBP wait time 🕐

Mexico / United States

5a Secondary inspection

6 State-specific commercial vehicle safety inspection

5b Nonintrusive inspection

① Queue for Mexican customs	② Mexican customs	③ Queue for U.S. primary inspection	④ Primary inspection
U.S.-bound commercial vehicles wait for processing at Mexican customs. Measurement of a vehicle's "total crossing time" begins here.	Prior to entering the United States commercial vehicles are cleared by Mexican customs agents. When the vehicle is cleared, it crosses the border and proceeds to the Customs and Border Protection (CBP) primary inspection facility in the United States.	CBP's definition of wait time begins when a commercial vehicle arrives at the end of the queue for primary inspection.	CBP's definition of wait time ends as soon as the vehicle arrives at the primary inspection booth. At a primary inspection booth, a U.S.-bound commercial vehicle makes its first contact with CBP officers who review documentation on the exporter, importer, and goods being transported. If its documentation is consistent with CBP requirements and no further inspections are required, the vehicle is allowed to pass through the port without further inspection. However, CBP may direct the vehicle to secondary inspection depending upon the cargo, law enforcement requirements, or officer initiative.

5a Secondary inspection	5b Nonintrusive inspection	6 State-specific commercial vehicle safety inspection	⑦ Exit
Secondary inspection involves more detailed document and physical examination, possibly including manual offloading and inspection by CBP or other federal agencies. For example, Food and Drug Administration inspectors may request commercial vehicles be sent to secondary inspection to ensure compliance with U.S. safety requirements.	CBP officers who suspect a commercial vehicle to hold persons or contraband can refer the vehicle to be scanned by gamma ray systems or advanced radiation portal monitors.	At some crossings, commercial vehicles may be inspected by federal and state departments of transportation to ensure compliance with federal and state-specific safety standards.	Once the truck has been cleared by CBP, other federal agencies, and any state department of transportation inspectors, it is allowed to proceed freely into the United States. The measurement of a vehicle's "total crossing time" ends here.

Source: GAO analysis of CBP data.

GAO-13-603 U.S.-Mexico Border

To facilitate the travel of low-risk screened shipments across the border, CBP created the FAST program, which is intended to secure and facilitate legitimate trade by providing expedited processing of participants' merchandise in designated traffic lanes at select border crossings, fewer referrals to secondary inspections, "front-of-the-line" processing for CBP secondary inspections, and enhanced security.[20] To be eligible to receive the benefits of the FAST program, every link in the supply chain—the carrier, the importer, and the manufacturer—is required to be certified under the Customs and Trade Partnership Against Terrorism (C-TPAT) program and the driver must be preapproved for participation in the FAST program.[21]

CBP Public Reporting of Border Crossing Wait Time Data

CBP defines border wait time as the time it takes for a vehicle to travel from the end of the queue—which may be in Mexico or the United States, depending on the length of the line—to the CBP primary inspection point in the United States. See figure 2 for an illustration of these points in the border-crossing process. As a service to the traveling public and the trade community, CBP began publicly reporting hourly wait time data through a web page on CBP.gov in early 2004, and currently reports these data for 42 of 46 crossings on the southwest border. CBP began formally collecting commercial and private passenger vehicle wait times on a daily basis in late September 2001 in response to the delays experienced immediately after September 11, 2001, when heightened enforcement efforts resulted in significant delays at many land border ports of entry. Over time, the collection of wait time data evolved as additional crossings were added and the amount of information collected was expanded. CBP reported that it is important that the trade community have current and consistent wait times on the CBP web site, noting that the web site is the only source of wait time information at many locations.

---

[20]Front-of-the-line processing refers to opportunities at some crossings for FAST vehicles to begin their secondary inspection before non-FAST vehicles when there is a backup of traffic waiting for secondary inspection.

[21]C-TPAT is a customs-to-business partnership program that provides benefits to supply chain companies that agree to comply with predetermined security measures.

Some border stakeholders, such as those in the private sector, find "total crossing time" to be a more useful measure than CBP's definition of wait time. Unlike CBP's narrower "wait time" measure, which captures the time it takes for a vehicle to travel from the end of the queue to the CBP primary inspection point, total crossing time is generally defined as the total time elapsed from entering the line in Mexico leading to Mexican export inspection through exit from U.S. inspection facilities, including any U.S. state-conducted inspections. See figure 2 for an illustration of the differences between these two measurements.

CBP Staff at Land Border Crossings

CBP has developed a workload staffing model to determine the optimum number of CBP officers that each port of entry needs to accomplish its mission responsibilities at its land, air, and sea ports of entry. This model existed in different versions, beginning in fiscal year 2006. The conference report for the fiscal year 2007 DHS appropriations act, expressing concern regarding CBP's ability to align staffing resources to mission requirements, directed CBP to submit a resource allocation model for staffing requirements that would explain CBP's methodology for aligning staffing levels with threats, vulnerabilities, and workload across all mission areas.[22] In April 2013, CBP submitted the most recent version of its workload staffing model to Congress in response to language in the conference and committee reports for the fiscal year 2012 DHS appropriations.[23]

DHS has received appropriations to support increased staffing levels for CBP officers on the southwest border over the last 5 fiscal years. For example, the conference report accompanying the fiscal year 2009 supplemental appropriation indicated that it included $30 million to fund the hiring of up to 125 CBP officers for the southwest border, and the fiscal year 2010 emergency supplemental appropriation for border

---

[22]H.R. Rep. No. 109-699, at 126 (2006) (Conf. Rep.). The explanatory statement for the fiscal year 2008 consolidated appropriations act noted that CBP had submitted the resource allocation model and had developed a workload staffing model to generate estimates of staffing needed to meet workload and mission requirements.

[23]H.R. Rep. No. 112-331, at 958 (2011) (Conf. Rep.); H.R. Rep. No. 112-91, at 27-28 (2011); S. Rep. No. 112-74, at 31 (2011).

security included $29 million for hiring additional CBP officers for southwest border land ports of entry.[24]

Assessments of Port Infrastructure

CBP and GSA have assessed infrastructure needs at all land border crossings over the last 9 fiscal years. From fiscal years 2004 to 2006, CBP assessed its complete portfolio of land port of entry facilities and identified infrastructure investment needs through its SRA process. The SRA includes architectural and analytical assessments of land port of entry inspection facilities' condition and operations as well as relevant regional planning data and studies. Appendix III provides more information regarding CBP's SRA process.

GSA has also assessed land port of entry infrastructure needs when planning and designing land port of entry renovation projects. For example, before undertaking construction, GSA evaluates the design of projects to renovate, expand, or construct a new land port of entry using its BorderWizard™ program—a program used to simulate projected traffic flow through the proposed facility to help identify potential deficiencies, such as insufficient primary inspection lanes.[25] See appendix IV for more information on completed, ongoing, or planned infrastructure improvement projects at southwest border land ports of entry for fiscal years 2008 through 2012.

---

[24]H.R. Rep. No. 111-151, at 110 (2009) (Conf. Rep.); Pub. L. No. 111-230, 124 Stat. 2485, 2485 (2010).

[25]BorderWizard™ analyses include factors such as projected traffic volume, workload processing time, and the proposed infrastructure improvements. The analysis does not take into account staffing levels at the port of entry.

CBP's Wait Time Data Are Unreliable for Informing the Public and CBP Management Decisions, and CBP Has Not Assessed the Feasibility of Automated Data Collection Options

Wait Time Data Are Unreliable and of Limited Usefulness; CBP Has Not Taken Steps to Improve Its Current Wait Time Estimation Methodology

CBP policy identifies two methodologies to be used by ports of entry for manually calculating wait times for commercial vehicles; however, challenges in implementing these methodologies contribute to CBP wait time data being of limited usefulness for public reporting and management decision making across border crossings. Specifically, CBP policy provides port directors two options for manually calculating wait times at the border crossings they oversee: (1) line-of-sight and (2) driver survey. Port directors for each crossing are to choose which methodology to use based primarily on a consideration of the infrastructure layout of each crossing. CBP officers at border crossings are to use the first methodology when the end of the line is visible via the naked eye or camera. In accordance with this methodology, the CBP supervisor at the crossing is to estimate wait time based on traffic volume, number of lanes open, and where the end of the queue occurs relative to landmarks (i.e., foot of bridge, building, or intersection). When the end of the line is not visible, CBP policy recommends that officials estimate wait times using the second methodology—asking at least five drivers how long they have been waiting in the queue, dropping the highest and lowest responses, and averaging the rest.

CBP's October 2007 interim guidance, which prescribes these two methodologies to calculate wait times, states that "it is critically important that all locally posted wait times for ports or crossings are reasonably accurate and are uniformly reported by all stakeholders." In addition, CBP's May 2008 memorandum on land border wait time measurement states that "the importance of accurate land border wait time measures cannot be understated. Efficient and reliable land border wait time measures help to facilitate the movement of people and goods across our border and directly impact the economic health of border communities and the nation as a whole." Among the six crossings we visited, Mariposa used driver surveys, and the remaining five crossings used line of sight to estimate wait times. However, CBP's wait time data are of limited usefulness for public reporting and management decision making across border crossings because of three key factors: (1) CBP officers inconsistently implemented the line-of-sight methodology; (2) the other CBP-approved methodology, driver surveys, is inherently unreliable; and (3) CBP officials use different methodologies to calculate wait times across land border crossings.[26]

Inconsistent implementation of line-of-sight methodology: Port directors at the five crossings we visited that primarily used the line-of-sight methodology cited implementation challenges resulting in data that are not reliable for management decisions and informing the public.[27] Specifically:

- At all five of the crossings, the end of the queue at times extended beyond the landmarks used in the line-of-sight methodology and none had a camera system in place with the capacity to consistently view the end of queues. Two crossings—World Trade Bridge and Columbia Solidarity Bridge—had camera systems that allowed officials to view the queue several miles into Mexico, but CBP officers noted that it could not be used to see the end of the queue on hazy and dusty days. CBP previously reported in a fiscal year 2008 WHTI program office study on the reliability of CBP's methods for calculating commercial vehicle wait times that if officials cannot see the end of the line, they cannot accurately gauge the full duration of wait times.

- At two crossings—World Trade Bridge and Columbia Solidarity Bridge—senior field office and port officials noted that there were frequently gaps between groups of trucks in the queue and that at one of these crossings trucks comingled with private cars on the bridge

---

[26]CBP officials responsible for maintaining CBP's wait time data and others noted that they do not maintain information on the wait time calculation methodologies used at each crossing. They reported that they would have to ask officials at each crossing to develop such a list.

[27]CBP officials at three of the five crossings that reported primarily using the line-of-sight methodology also reported using the driver survey methodology at times, such as during construction or to routinely check their line-of-sight methodology.

leading up to the primary inspection booths for commercial traffic. According to these officials, these factors hinder officers' ability to accurately determine the full duration of wait times as gaps or cars between commercial vehicles may make wait times appear to be longer or shorter than they actually are.

- At one crossing—Otay Mesa—CBP officers used the line-of-sight methodology but did not consider the number of primary inspection lanes open, as required by CBP policy.[28] The number of lanes open to commercial vehicle traffic influences the rate at which traffic moves through primary inspection. CBP's fiscal year 2008 WHTI study on the reliability of CBP's methods for calculating commercial vehicle wait times notes that the number of lanes open greatly affects wait time, so not considering the number of lanes open limits CBP's ability to accurately estimate wait times using the line-of-sight methodology.

Driver survey methodology is unreliable: CBP's fiscal year 2008 WHTI study on the reliability of CBP's methods for calculating commercial vehicle wait times stated that driver surveys have been shown to be consistently inaccurate when measuring wait time in part because they measure the wait time of travelers currently at the front of the queue, not the expected wait time of travelers currently at the end of the queue. As a result, if queuing conditions quickly change, the wait times collected using this methodology become inaccurate. In addition, Port officials at Mariposa used driver surveys as the crossing's primary method of estimating wait times, but noted that the methodology produced unreliable wait time data. Senior CBP officials at this crossing reported that officers had to use driver surveys to estimate wait times because a curve in the road leading up to the crossing obstructs officers' view of the queue, thereby preventing the crossing from using the line-of-sight approach. Senior CBP officials at this crossing stated that driver survey is an unreliable methodology because of survey bias—drivers may be inclined to report longer or shorter wait times than they actually experienced.

Different methodologies across land border crossings: Port directors choose between the two CBP-approved methodologies to estimate wait times in accordance with CBP policy; however, OFO and OA headquarters officials stated that the use of different methodologies at

---

[28]CBP officials at Otay Mesa did not respond to our question about why the number of primary inspection lanes was not considered.

crossings precludes comparison of data across locations in making management decisions. Although officials at each crossing determine which of the two methodologies to use based on the layout of each crossing and other local characteristics, the use of different methodologies at crossings makes CBP's wait time data unreliable for comparison across southwest border crossings, as they may produce different results. OFO and OA headquarters officials told us that because of the different methodologies used at different crossings, the wait time data are not comparable across crossings and therefore are of limited use in making resource allocation decisions.

In light of these challenges in implementing CBP's approved methodologies for estimating wait times, CBP's wait time data do not allow for reliable trend analysis to show the extent of wait times within or across southwest border crossings. Industry representatives at two of the six crossings we visited reported that, in their view, the actual wait times commercial vehicle drivers experienced were often longer than those CBP publicly reported. For example, industry representatives at the roundtable we convened in Nogales reported their view that wait times, as defined by CBP, were at times up to 2 hours longer than those CBP publicly reported. Industry representatives at two other crossings reported that CBP's wait time data were generally accurate.[29] In addition, three organizations that commissioned studies to quantify the economic impact of wait times at southwest border crossings did not use CBP's wait time data as the basis for their studies but rather collected original wait time data by, for example, using cameras to photograph trucks' license plates at various points along the border-crossing routes and then matching these photographs to identify the wait time of each vehicle. (See appendix I for the results of these studies.) Because of these various limitations, we and others cannot use CBP's wait time data to analyze the extent of current wait times across border crossings on the southwest border or determine historical trends.

Wait time data currently reported on CBP's public website are of limited usefulness to inform industry and the public because of the data

---

[29]Officials at these two crossings noted that CBP's wait time data are of limited usefulness because they do not capture total crossing time. Industry representatives we met with at the remaining two of six crossings indicated the need for a standardized system for wait time measurement but did not specifically indicate whether CBP's wait time data were longer or shorter than actual waits they experienced.

limitations we identified and because they do not reflect the total border crossing time. None of the industry stakeholders representing 21 companies and associations we met with over the course of our study reported using CBP's wait time data because they questioned the accuracy of the data. Industry representatives at the roundtables we convened in Nogales, San Diego, and Laredo said that more reliable wait time data would be useful to, for example, help businesses improve the efficiency of their operations and to make informed decisions including where to build new facilities, how much inventory to maintain, when and how frequently to send shipments across the border, and when to schedule truckers' or manufacturing plant employees' shifts. In addition, industry representatives at our roundtables in El Paso and San Diego noted that they did not use CBP's wait time data because the data did not provide information on the duration of the complete border-crossing experience—total crossing time—a more comprehensive measure that would be helpful in making business decisions.[30] A 2008 study commissioned by the Department of Commerce also found it was important to use a measure of total crossing time to capture the border-crossing system as a whole, and to account for the fact that wait time associated with U.S. primary inspection was not the sole driver of total wait time for commercial vehicles. Instead, they reported that delays were due to several factors, including many outside U.S. federal control. FHWA officials acknowledge the value of total crossing time and are piloting projects to automate such data collection.

In addition, according to CBP headquarters officials, these wait time data are also not sufficiently reliable to inform CBP management decisions—more specifically, decisions on staffing and infrastructure investments—and officers at the six crossings we visited told us that they use the wait time data in limited ways. At the headquarters level, OFO officials stated that because of data limitations, CBP's wait time data are not useful for comparison across crossings and explained that they do not use the data as a basis for determining staffing needs or allocating staff across field offices but rather rely on CBP's traffic volume data as a proxy.[31] A senior

---

[30]CBP officials report that industry's interest in total crossing time may present an opportunity for CBP to engage in a public-private partnership.

[31]According to CBP officials and documents, CBP's workload staffing model does not (1) consider CBP's current wait time data as an input, or (2) assume a certain wait time goal because the model is not designed to calculate different results depending on performance-related goals, such as meeting wait time service goals.

OFO human capital official explained that the wait time data are not systematically compared across ports but ports with known chronic wait time problems do get consideration in staff allocation decisions. Similarly, OA headquarters officials stated that they do not use wait time data to prioritize infrastructure improvement projects because of concerns about the reliability of CBP's wait time data. However, CBP field office and port officials reported using their existing wait time data to a limited extent to inform management decisions in the field. Specifically, senior CBP officials at the six crossings we visited reported using wait time data as one of various factors considered when, for example, allocating staff across crossings and shifts, overtime decisions, and as support for white papers sent to headquarters requesting funding for infrastructure improvement projects. CBP officials at the six crossings we visited reported that more reliable wait time data would be useful to them in making such decisions. For example, CBP officials at each of these crossings stated that more reliable wait time data would help them in making staffing decisions.

CBP does not have efforts underway or planned to help port officials overcome challenges to consistent implementation of existing wait time estimation methodologies. For example, CBP has not fully implemented recommendations from a fiscal year 2008 CBP study that could help the agency implement its current wait time estimation methodologies more reliably. In fiscal year 2008, CBP's WHTI program office studied the reliability of CBP's methods for calculating commercial vehicle wait times and identified six recommendations, three of which could, in part, help address the limitations discussed above. The recommendations directed CBP to, among other things (1) use closed-circuit television cameras to measure wait time in real time; (2) provide a standardized measurement and validation tool, such as a useful and well-documented benchmarking system; and (3) continue to monitor and evaluate applications of transportation technologies at the border that allow for better measurement and reporting of wait times.[32] CBP headquarters officials from three offices—the office that sponsored the report (Land Border Integration), the office in charge of cargo operations (Cargo Conveyance and Security), and the office that maintains the agency's wait time data (Planning Program Analysis and Evaluation)—were all unclear as to the steps, if any, that had been taken to address the first two recommendations and which office was responsible for implementing them. With regard to the first recommendation, an official we met with in Cargo Conveyance and Security said that some crossings had access to cameras that helped them view the end of the line, but this official did not know how many crossings on the southern border had cameras for this purpose and further stated that there were no plans to expand camera availability to improve wait time data reliability. With regard to the second recommendation, this Cargo Conveyance and Security official stated that CBP had not taken steps to develop a standardized wait time measurement and validation tool and had no plans to do so. However, CBP officials with Land Border Integration and Planning, Program Analysis, and Evaluation stated that CBP had implemented the third recommendation by continuing to monitor and evaluate applications of transportation technologies in its work with FHWA to pilot projects for automating data collection.

CBP guidance identifies the importance of reliable wait time measurement to facilitate the movement of people and goods across the border. Further, *Standards for Internal Control in the Federal Government* calls for agencies to establish controls, such as those provided through policies and procedures, to ensure the accuracy and timeliness of data. Control activities that ensure the prompt, complete, and accurate recording of data help to maintain their relevance and value to

---

[32]In making the first recommendation, the report notes that for various geographical reasons it is often difficult for cameras positioned on the U.S. side to provide adequate views of queues. Therefore, the report recommends that, where possible, CBP work to leverage use of cameras in use by stakeholders on or near land border crossings. With regard to the second recommendation to provide a standardized measurement and validation tool, the report further specifies that such a tool could include a spreadsheet with formulas taking into account the local benchmarks used to identify the end of the line, the number of inbound lanes, the average processing time, and the number of open primary booths, among other variables, in order to determine wait time. The report also included three other recommendations including the following: (1) provide administrative support to ensure accurate wait time reporting and reduce CBP officer workload, (2) increase the timeliness and frequency of wait time updates on CBP's website to a minimum of 30 minutes or less, and (3) provide video feeds to the CBP website.

management in controlling operations and making decisions. In the near term, identifying and carrying out steps that can be taken to help CBP officials overcome challenges to consistent implementation of existing wait time estimation methodologies—such as implementing past CBP recommendations to expand the use of cameras to see the ends of queues and providing standardized wait time measurement and validation tools—could improve the reliability and usefulness of CBP's current wait time data.

CBP Has Not Assessed the Feasibility of New Automation Options

In February 2008, FHWA, in coordination with state DOTs and CBP, initiated pilot projects to develop automated wait time data collection methods at select southwest border crossings. Automation of wait time data collection relies on Radio-Frequency Identification readers to read the unique signals from passing vehicles at several points along the border-crossing route. These data points are then automatically matched and analyzed to estimate the current wait time at that crossing. As of March 2013, FHWA and state DOTs in Arizona, California, and Texas had eight pilot projects under way or completed to automate and standardize calculation of both wait time and total crossing time at eight crossings on the southwest border, including projects at each of the six crossings we visited.[33] Wait time data resulting from some of these pilots is currently shared on a publicly available website with updates every 10 minutes.[34] These eight projects were initiated on a crossing-by-crossing basis and are in various stages of implementation—one completed and seven ongoing. Two additional projects are planned so senior FHWA officials expect automated wait time data to be available at 10 crossings by 2015 at which point current federal funding commitments for these projects end.[35]

CBP headquarters and field officials, as well as FHWA and a Texas Department of Transportation official, cited a range of potential benefits

[33]The completed pilot project was at Otay Mesa (Otay Mesa, California) and the ongoing projects are at Pharr (Pharr, Texas), Bridge of the Americas (El Paso, Texas), Ysleta (El Paso, Texas), World Trade Bridge (Laredo, Texas), Columbia Solidarity Bridge (Laredo, Texas), Veterans (Brownsville, Texas), and Mariposa (Nogales, Arizona).

[34]The website is http://bcis.tamu.edu.

[35]Automation projects are planned at Santa Teresa (Santa Teresa, New Mexico) and Camino Real International Bridge (Eagle Pass, Texas).

that could result from automating border wait time measurement. CBP's fiscal year 2008 WHTI report found that the long-term solution to standardize wait time measurement is to take advantage of automation technology. CBP headquarters, field office, and port officials told us that automation would reduce the burden on staff of manually collecting wait time data and increase staff availability for security efforts and other tasks. OFO headquarters officials also stated that automation would increase the accuracy, reliability, and timeliness of the wait time data that are collected and disseminated. Moreover, they stated that automated data would come from a more independent source, and thus the data may be perceived by industry organizations as more accurate than CBP's current data. This would reduce the burden on CBP officials to respond to queries about their wait time data, according to CBP officials. OFO headquarters officials and senior CBP officials at the six crossings we visited reported that accurate wait time data would facilitate CBP management decisions such as staffing needs, infrastructure investment, performance management (such as evaluating efforts to mitigate wait times), and operations planning at land ports of entry. In addition, CBP officials at four of the six crossings reported automation could provide data on CBP's definition of wait time as well as total border-crossing time. This could provide CBP with more holistic information on the complete border-crossing experience, thereby improving CBP's ability to identify and address bottlenecks and providing industry stakeholders with more useful data to inform their business processes.

At the same time, CBP officials reported limitations of the current automation pilot projects. In 2011, CBP commissioned a study to review the quality of the data resulting from the Texas-based pilot projects and found the automated wait time data were not yet sufficiently accurate for CBP's purposes. In response to these findings, CBP worked with pilot project officials to modify the algorithm used to calculate the wait times, with the intention to improve the accuracy of the data. Another concern raised by CBP officials is that none of the pilots are yet able to consistently differentiate between wait times for FAST and non-FAST traffic. Not capturing separate wait time data for FAST and non-FAST traffic could limit the usefulness for key industry stakeholders and limit CBP's ability to measure whether FAST participants are experiencing reduced wait times, as set forth in FAST program goals. FHWA officials reported that the technology solutions used in the current pilot projects are flexible enough to enable adding more readers to differentiate results for FAST and non-FAST traffic, but none of the current pilot projects are gathering data for this purpose, and FHWA officials reported that they have no plans to conduct additional research on solutions that differentiate between FAST and non-FAST traffic. In addition, CBP officials note that there are no pilot programs to automate wait time data collection at 34 of the 42 southwest border crossings where CBP currently reports hourly wait times.

CBP, as the lead agency in collecting and reporting wait time data and the sole source of wait time data across the southwest border, does not have plans to oversee or manage these automation projects, although FHWA and others are anticipating an expanded CBP role once the pilot phases conclude. FHWA officials have led the research phase of these projects but expect their role to decline as the pilot phases end, and they are looking to others to manage these efforts in the longer term. FHWA has taken a lead role in the research, testing, and evaluation of wait time automation technology including fully funding the pilot projects at the Bridge of the Americas and Otay Mesa and providing limited financial support for others. However, FHWA officials stated that they do not plan to fund these projects after the pilot phases end. CBP has coordinated with FHWA by, for example, consulting on the algorithms used to project wait times, but CBP has not provided funding for the projects on the southwest border. CBP officials reported that they do not intend to fund, adopt, or otherwise oversee these wait time automation projects once the pilot phases supported by FHWA and state DOTs conclude because CBP officials stated that they want another entity, such as FHWA or state DOTs, to do so. Texas Department of Transportation officials report that they are committed to continuing the Texas-based pilot projects in the short term, but are looking for another source of funding, possibly CBP or others to support the projects in the future. There are no other such commitments for the pilots in other states. CBP officials report that they are in discussion with FHWA about collaborative approaches to continuing these efforts, such as public-private partnerships.

CBP officials stated that the agency has not taken action to improve or modify its current methods for collecting and reporting wait time data in the short-term because officials believe that automated collection of wait time data is the most effective way to obtain reliable, standardized data, and the current automation projects are still in development. However, CBP has not assessed the feasibility of replacing or supplementing current methods of manually calculating wait times with the automated methods piloted by DOT or other means. Assessing the feasibility could include assessing all of the associated costs and benefits, options for how the agency will use and publicly report the results of automated data collection, the potential trade-offs associated with moving to this new system, and other factors such as those influencing the possible expansion of automation efforts to the 34 other locations that currently report wait times but have no automation project under way. OFO officials stated that CBP has not considered assessing the feasibility of automating wait time data collection and does not have estimates of potential costs or time frames because the pilot projects are still in development and CBP management has not committed to automating wait time data collection. However, standards for program management call for the feasibility of programs to be assessed early on.[36] Given that CBP officials have stated that automated data collection is the most effective method for obtaining standardized and reliable wait time data, conducting an assessment of the feasibility of the methods piloted by FHWA or other automation methods, in consultation with FHWA and state DOTs, could help CBP determine how to best achieve its goal of improving the reliability of its publicly reported wait time data.

CBP Analyses and Officials Identified Some Infrastructure and Staff Needs, but the Methodology Used to Allocate Staff across Ports of Entry Has Not Been Documented

---

[36]Project Management Institute, *The Standard for Program Management©*, Second Edition.

CBP Analyses and Officials Indicated Need for Additional Infrastructure at Some Crossings, and Our Analysis of Data on Primary Lane Use Generally Supported These Assessments

CBP analyses and port officials identified needs for additional infrastructure—such as more lanes—at some border crossings, and our analysis of CBP data on lane use generally supported agency views on the extent to which CBP opens lanes at the six crossings we visited. Further, our analysis supports CBP officials' statements that they generally open and close primary inspection lanes in response to fluctuations in commercial traffic volume, but some port officials cited constraints to opening more lanes during times of peak traffic.

CBP and GSA assessments and officials identified current infrastructure limitations affecting commercial vehicle processing at three of the six crossings we visited. Specifically, CBP and GSA assessments and CBP officials cited infrastructure limitations related to an insufficient number of primary lanes at Otay Mesa, insufficient space for secondary inspections at Otay Mesa and World Trade Bridge, and poor facility layout as well as an insufficient number of exit gates at Bridge of the Americas.[37] CBP port of entry officials for two of the three remaining crossings we visited stated that current infrastructure was sufficient to process commercial traffic at Columbia Solidarity Bridge and Ysleta. At the last crossing, Mariposa, CBP port officials reported that infrastructure would be sufficient once GSA's ongoing project to replace and expand the port is completed in the fall of 2014. Table 1 summarizes the infrastructure needs identified in CBP or GSA assessments as well as those identified by CBP port officials at the six crossings we visited.

---

[37]Upon arriving at the border crossing, traffic waiting to enter the United States queues up in primary inspection lanes that lead to primary inspection booths where a CBP officer reviews documentation on the exporter, importer, and goods being transported. If no further inspections are required, the vehicle is allowed to enter the United States. Secondary inspections occur when a vehicle is referred by the primary line officer for further inspection, including gamma ray scans, paperwork, and physical examinations.

Table 1: Infrastructure Needs as Identified in Customs and Border Protection (CBP) and General Services Administration Assessments (GSA) and by CBP Officials at the Six Crossings We Visited

Name and location of border crossings	Infrastructure needs identified in CBP or GSA assessments and reported actions taken to address these needs	Infrastructure needs identified by CBP port officials
Otay Mesa: San Diego, CA	GSA assessments conducted in 2008 and 2010 predicted that commercial vehicle wait times would increase because of deficiencies including inadequate primary lanes and space to conduct secondary and nonintrusive inspections.[a] These most recent assessments found that eight additional primary lanes were needed to meet the demands of projected commercial traffic volume at the crossing.	CBP port officials reported there is an insufficient number of primary lanes and there is insufficient secondary inspection space.
Mariposa: Nogales, AZ	CBP's 2005 Strategic Resource Assessment (SRA) identified the need for additional secondary inspection space, and a 2009 GSA assessment identified the need for additional primary inspection lanes, among other deficiencies identified. Four primary lanes were added in April 2012.	CBP port officials told us that once the ongoing renovation and expansion project is complete in fall 2014, Mariposa will have no further infrastructure needs for commercial vehicle processing.
Bridge of the Americas: El Paso, TX	CBP's 2006 SRA found that the crossing was poorly configured and that the configuration and placement of primary inspection lanes and exit gates created backups and bottlenecks that prevented the effective flow of both regular commercial traffic and Free and Secure Trade traffic.[b] Two new exit booths were added in 2012 to partially address these issues.[c] CBP and GSA officials have not conducted an assessment to determine the extent of reconfiguration needed, stating that they conduct such assessments when funds become available to do so.	CBP port officials reported the Bridge of the Americas currently has sufficient capacity at its primary and secondary inspection facilities, but that the crossing's layout and number of exit gates adversely affect the flow of traffic. They also stated that the crossing is at maximum capacity and if commercial traffic increases, as CBP officials expect, the crossing will have an insufficient number of primary inspection lanes and insufficient infrastructure for secondary inspections.
Ysleta: El Paso, TX	CBP's 2006 SRA identified an inadequate number of primary inspection lanes to process commercial traffic during peak times and reported that the placement of exit gates contributes to congestion within the facility. These deficiencies were addressed when GSA completed a renovation that included adding two primary inspection lanes in October 2008 and reconfiguring the site.	CBP port officials stated that the port had a sufficient number of primary lanes and sufficient infrastructure for secondary inspections to process commercial traffic.
Columbia Solidarity Bridge: Laredo, TX	CBP's 2006 SRA did not identify any infrastructure deficiencies that would limit the crossing's ability to process commercial traffic.	CBP port officials stated that the crossing had a sufficient primary and secondary capacity to process commercial traffic.
World Trade Bridge: Laredo, TX	CBP's 2006 SRA reported a need to expand primary and secondary inspection infrastructure. Seven primary inspection lanes were added in 2011; CBP and GSA officials have not conducted an assessment to determine the extent to which secondary facilities need to be expanded. CBP and GSA officials stated that they conduct such assessments when funds become available to do so.	CBP port officials stated that seven primary lanes were added in 2011, but insufficient space to conduct secondary and nonintrusive inspections results in congestion.

Source: GAO analysis of CBP and GSA documents and CBP officials' statements.

Notes: Primary inspections are conducted by a CBP officer at a primary inspection booth. Secondary inspections occur when a vehicle is referred for further inspection, including gamma ray scans, paperwork, and physical examinations.

[a]Nonintrusive inspection includes the use of gamma ray technologies to detect contraband in commercial trucks.

[b]CBP initiated the Free and Secure Trade (FAST) program in 2002 to expedite the travel of known low-risk screened shipments across the border. Seventeen out of the 24 land border crossings on the southwest border have dedicated FAST lanes to expedite FAST traffic.

[c]According to CBP officials, this infrastructure improvement project at the Bridge of the Americas was funded out of the Office of Field Operations' operating budget at a cost of approximately $264,500.

Further, our analysis of CBP data on lane use generally supported CBP officials' statements regarding the extent to which CBP officials open existing primary inspection lanes at the six crossings we visited. The number of primary inspection lanes available and open at each crossing was frequently cited by CBP and industry officials as a critical variable affecting wait times for commercial vehicles and, further, as evidence of whether a crossing's primary lane infrastructure was sufficient to process current traffic volumes. For example, at all the locations we visited, industry representatives expressed concern that CBP had an insufficient number of primary inspection lanes to process current traffic volumes or was not fully utilizing existing lanes.[38] To determine the extent to which CBP was opening its existing primary inspection lanes, we analyzed CBP data on the average hourly percentage of primary inspection lanes open per month during operating hours over the last 5 fiscal years (October 2007-September 2012). This analysis showed the following:

- In fiscal year 2012, lane use data for two of the six crossings we visited suggest that these crossings—Otay Mesa and Mariposa—were at times operating at or near full capacity, as reported by agency officials. In fiscal year 2012, Otay Mesa opened an hourly average of 82 to 89 percent of its primary inspection lanes per month. At Mariposa, our analysis of lane use data for the first half of fiscal year 2012, prior to the addition of four new primary inspection lanes in April 2012, showed that during months of peak traffic, port officials opened

---

[38]For example, industry representatives and Mexican officials in Laredo, Texas told us that seven new primary inspection lanes were added at the World Trade Bridge in 2011 to reduce wait times for commercial vehicles, but the new lanes were often not opened.

an hourly average of between 80 and 84 percent of Mariposa's primary lanes per month.[39]

- The average hourly percentage of primary lanes open per month at the remaining four crossings we visited—Bridge of the Americas, Ysleta, Columbia Solidarity Bridge, and World Trade Bridge—were all lower.[40] This generally supported CBP officials' statements that they have the capacity to open more primary inspection lanes at these crossings.

Our analysis also supports CBP officials' statements that they generally open and close primary inspection lanes in response to fluctuations in commercial traffic volume—a practice CBP calls active lane management; however, some port officials cited constraints in opening more lanes during times of peak traffic. Port officials at all six crossings we visited reported that they consider commercial traffic volume, among other factors, when deciding to open and close primary inspection lanes. We compared trends in CBP's data on lane use and commercial traffic volume and found that the two were generally consistent at five of the six crossings we visited, supporting CBP officers' statements that they generally open more lanes when traffic volume rises and close lanes when traffic decreases.[41] However, CBP officials at one of these five crossings—World Trade Bridge—explained that other factors kept them from opening all primary inspection lanes during periods of high traffic. Specifically, these officials said that bottlenecks would form if all primary

---

[39]Mariposa is a major crossing for agricultural products and therefore has high seasonal variability in commercial traffic volume. Prior to the addition of new primary inspection lanes, the peak months in fiscal year 2012 were January, February, March, and April, when average monthly commercial vehicle traffic volume exceeded that of nonpeak months by approximately 20 percent. The monthly average percentage of lanes opened on average per hour for the nonpeak months in fiscal year 2012, prior to the opening of new lanes on April, 30 2012—October 2011 to December 2011—ranged from 61 to 79 percent. Following the addition of new lanes in April 2012, this rate dropped to a monthly average of between 41 and 48 percent. However, it is important to note that this period (May-September 2012) is generally a period of low traffic volume, which, together with the availability of four new lanes, may account for this decrease.

[40]In fiscal year 2012, the average monthly percentage of primary lanes open on average per hour at these crossings was 39-79 percent at Bridge of the Americas, 27-48 percent at Ysleta, 36-38 percent at Columbia Solidarity Bridge, and 48-58 percent at World Trade Bridge.

[41]Our analysis does not indicate whether CBP is maximizing use of its lanes, but rather allows us to observe how closely the average hourly traffic volume per month corresponds to the average number of hourly lanes open per month.

lanes were opened, causing congestion throughout the facility because of limited space at secondary inspection.[42] The one crossing where the lane use and commercial traffic volume did not appear to track as closely was Columbia Solidarity Bridge. However, CBP officials at Columbia Solidarity Bridge explained that traffic volumes and wait times there were so low that they generally did not need to open or close lanes in response. Figure 3, an interactive graphic, summarizes our analysis and includes additional information for each of the six crossings we selected.

---

[42]In addition, CBP officials at the World Trade Bridge said they previously had insufficient staff to open all primary lanes during the midday rush but they have since added 20 new staff, which allowed them to add a new shift in January 2013 to minimize the effect of officer lunch breaks on their ability to open primary lanes. Because this initiative is relatively new, it is too early to assess its impact on lane utilization.

Figure 3: Average Hourly Traffic Volume and Average Hourly Percentage of Lanes Open Per Month at Selected Southwest Border Crossings, Fiscal Years 2008-2012

Click on the highlighted border crossings for more information. Click on the X to close. For a printer friendly version please see appendix V.

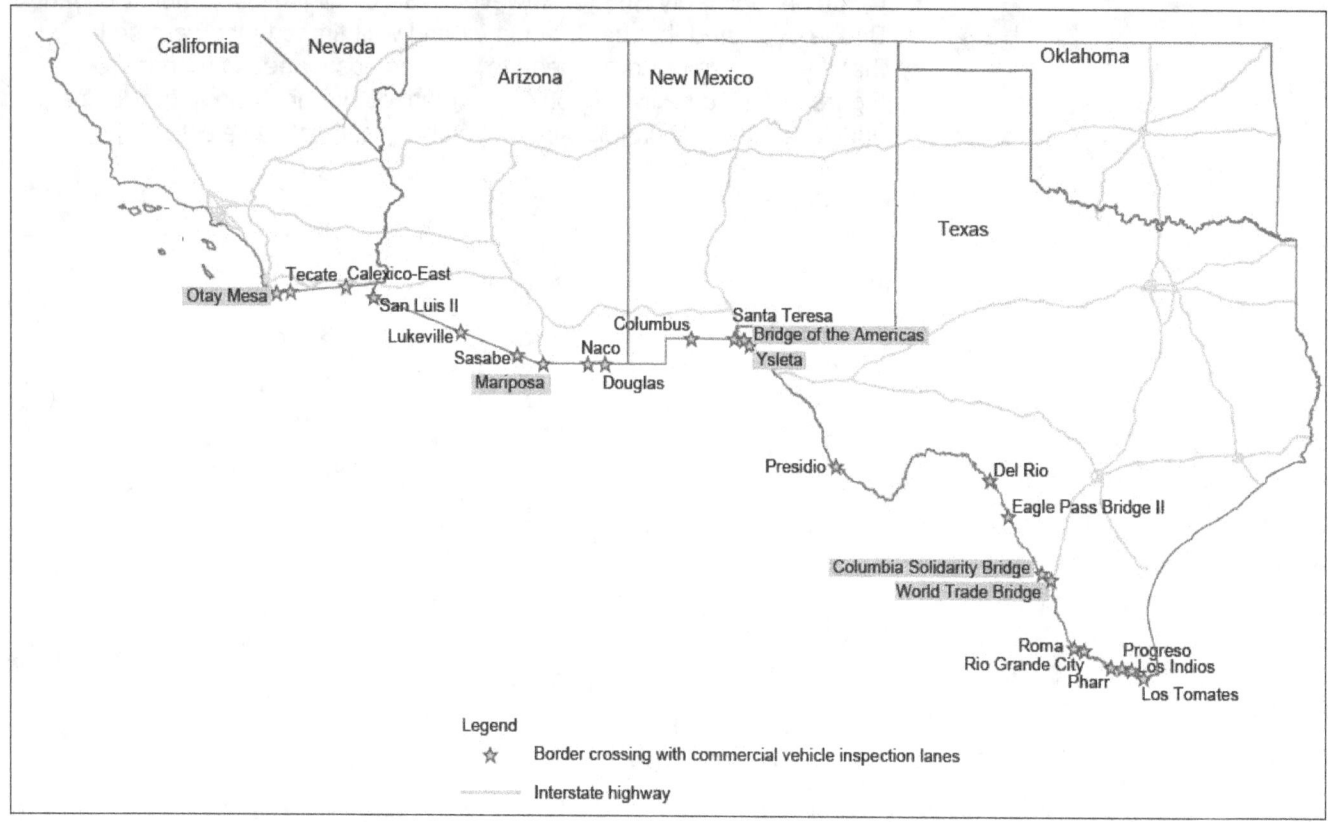

Source: GAO analysis of CBP data; CBP (photos).

CBP officials at headquarters and in the field cited various ways they are working to address infrastructure limitations given challenges caused by budgetary and geographic constraints, among others. In regard to budgetary constraints, CBP and GSA officials stated that GSA has not received funding to conduct additional expansion projects in the last 2 fiscal years, and as a result, they have not been able to execute new projects to address infrastructure needs at land ports of entry on the southwest border. GSA officials reported that the agency has used alternative funding sources to pay for prioritized infrastructure projects.[43] For example, GSA and CBP officials reported using funds from the city of Laredo to support the expansion of primary inspection lanes at the World Trade Bridge crossing in 2011.[44] In regard to geographic constraints, port officials at the Bridge of the Americas stated that the urban area around that crossing limits opportunities to expand the crossing's footprint. Officials with the city of El Paso told us that they are promoting a plan to divert all commercial traffic to the nearby Ysleta crossing because it has greater capacity to process commercial traffic and a larger footprint that can accommodate future expansion. CBP field office and port officials stated that they support this plan. In another example, CBP officials at headquarters and in the field reported participating in binational working groups in an effort to address the infrastructure limitations of ports of entry along the southwest border. For example, senior CBP officials reported participating in the U.S.-Mexico Joint Working Committee to develop regional master plans to better ensure the development of a well-coordinated land transportation and infrastructure planning process along the border.[45]

---

[43]According to GSA and CBP officials, GSA has statutory authority under 40 U.S.C. § 3175 to accept gifts from the private sector to fund expenses such as infrastructure renovation, but CBP does not have this authority. These officials also reported that GSA has accepted private sector gifts to fund the construction or renovation of land ports of entry.

[44]This primary lane expansion project was primarily funded by the city of Laredo. The city provided $7.5 million, GSA provided $1.3 million, and CBP provided $1.6 million.

[45]Regional border master plans are comprehensive long-range plans to identify and prioritize port of entry infrastructure needs and projects within a defined area. These plans represent binational stakeholder efforts to (1) prioritize port of entry and related transportation projects leading to ports of entry, (2) inform decision making, (3) allocate limited funding sources, and (4) ensure continued dialogue and coordination on future infrastructure needs and projects. In the near future, six regional border master plans will have been completed in California (1), Arizona (1), New Mexico (1), and Texas (3).

CBP Cites Need for Additional CBP Officers to Process Commercial Traffic at Some Crossings but Documentation Could Increase Transparency of Staff Allocations across Locations

CBP's workload staffing model—CBP's primary tool for determining the number of CBP officers needed at the nation's air, land, and sea ports—found that additional CBP officers are needed to meet CBP's mission requirements. CBP submitted the most recent version of its workload staffing model to Congress in response to language in the conference and committee reports for the fiscal year 2012 DHS appropriations.[46] According to CBP documents submitted to Congress, the workload staffing model found that 3,811 additional CBP officers are needed to meet CBP's mission requirements in fiscal year 2014.[47]

In addition, CBP field and port officials at three of the six crossings we visited reported having insufficient staff to process commercial traffic. Specifically, CBP field office and port officials reported insufficient staff at the World Trade Bridge, Columbia Solidarity Bridge, and Mariposa crossings and noted that insufficient staff at these crossings contributed to commercial vehicle wait times and reduced their ability to conduct secondary inspections, among other effects.[48] Officials at the remaining three crossings—Otay Mesa, Bridge of the Americas, and Ysleta—reported having a sufficient number of staff to process commercial traffic. However, senior OFO headquarters officials reported that all southwest

---

[46]H.R. Rep. No. 112-331, at 958 (2011) (Conf. Rep.); H.R. Rep. No. 112-91, at 27-28 (2011); S. Rep. No. 112-74, at 31 (2011) and Department of Homeland Security, U.S. Customs and Border Protection, *Resource Optimization at Ports of Entry: Fiscal Year 2012 Report to Congress* (Washington, D.C.: April 10, 2013).

[47] We did not evaluate CBP's workload staffing model as part of this review; however, we did review CBP documentation of the model. CBP officials and documentation indicated that the workload staffing model's purpose is to inform CBP budget decisions, such as the development of CBP budget requests, as well as its staffing allocation process. In addition, CBP documentation also indicated that the model's methodology assesses staffing needs based on workload data, processing times, and complexity. To arrive at the number of full-time-equivalent officers needed to complete the work, the model assumes a baseline number of hours per year are available for a CBP officer to focus on core mission work. The model then calculates the volume of core mission work using transactional data for each business process that CBP officers carry out—e.g., number of truck primary exams, number of truck container nonintrusive inspection exams, and so forth. CBP then uses data on the level of effort in minutes or hours expended each time an officer performs these activities to calculate the volume per hour, per inspection booth, per officer, and the equivalent officer hours to accomplish the mission.

[48]More specifically, CBP officials at these crossings told us that because of staffing shortages, they have had to reassign CBP officers from secondary inspection and other activities such as K-9 patrols to open additional primary lanes during periods of high traffic volume.

border land ports of entry require additional staff to perform at optimal levels.

CBP headquarters and field office officials cited efforts to mitigate the effect of reported staffing shortages on ports' ability to process commercial vehicle traffic. CBP officials reported that these staffing shortages, caused in part by budget constraints and the time needed to train and assign new CBP officers, challenged their ability to increase the numbers of officers at the ports of entry. Specifically, CBP officials reported that since fiscal year 2009, CBP has not received sufficient funding to hire the number of CBP officers that it requires at land ports of entry. In response to budgetary constraints, CBP headquarters officials reported working to identify alternative funding strategies as well as reviewing user fees to ensure they effectively support operations. For example, DHS's fiscal year 2014 congressional budget request included a proposed increase for 1,877 fee-funded full-time-equivalent positions in addition to a funding increase of approximately $210 million for 1,600 additional CBP officers. In response to staffing shortages related to the length of time it takes for new CBP officers to complete required training and to be available for duty at their assigned ports of entry, CBP headquarters officials reported considering the extent that new CBP officers have completed their training and are available for duty when allocating staff. They further reported actively working to adjust staff allocations across locations to better ensure that staffing levels are matched to areas of greatest need. For example, a senior OFO official reported prioritizing allocations to field offices with the highest discrepancy between current staffing levels and workload staffing model results when developing fiscal year 2012 annual staffing allocation. Finally, port officials at all six crossings we visited reported using overtime to mitigate the effect of any staffing shortages on ports' capacity to process commercial traffic. For example, port officials in El Paso said that using overtime pay was an effective and efficient solution to provide increased coverage to process commercial traffic during peak times on weekdays and on weekends.[49] However, officials at the Otay Mesa port of

---

[49]Officials with the Port of El Paso, for example, stated that Mexican and U.S. business practices generally result in peak times for commercial traffic that require increased staffing for only 2 hours or so in the morning and afternoon, but union requirements state that CBP officers must work in uninterrupted 8-hour shifts. Senior CBP officials also reported that the use of overtime allows coverage of peak times without hiring additional staff that are not needed to cover a full shift.

entry noted that the availability of overtime funds has decreased because of budget constraints in recent years.[50]

In fiscal year 2013, CBP revised its process to allocate available CBP officers to its field offices, ports of entry and border crossings. However, CBP has not yet documented this process or its methodology, including the factors and underlying rationale considered in making staff allocation decisions. A senior official in CBP's Human Capital Division reported that CBP's most recent staff allocation process consisted of the following six steps: (1) OFO's Human Capital Division obtained the workload staffing model's findings to determine the number of officers ideally needed to meet the expected workload; (2) Human Capital Division staff conducted a "gap analysis" by comparing the model's findings to current staff levels to identify the locations with the greatest gap between current and the staff levels identified by the workload staffing model; (3) Human Capital Division staff drafted a proposed staff allocation that realigned staff to those field offices with the greatest gap; (4) OFO leadership made adjustments to the proposal based on institutional priorities including mission, priorities, and threats before approving the allocation; (5) on receiving approval from leadership, OFO staff communicated the authorized staffing levels to each field office; and (6) the field offices then allocated their authorized staff to the individual ports of entry under their purview. However, this official explained that this process is not documented and there is no guidance clearly defining this methodology, the factors considered, or the rationale for making staff allocation decisions.

OFO Human Capital officials acknowledged the need to document this process and stated that they had not yet done so because, historically, such decisions were made informally and the current, more formalized process is still evolving. In addition, these officials noted that the last fiscal year was the first time OFO used the process described above and they planned to make further changes to the process within the next 2 fiscal years.

---

[50]CBP's Fiscal Year 2012 *Resource Optimization at Ports of Entry* report states that OFO's overtime budget has decreased by 8.2 percent from fiscal year 2008 through fiscal year 2013, thereby lessening the agency's ability to use overtime as a means of leveraging existing resources.

Best practices for strategic workforce planning identified by GAO emphasize the importance of ensuring that the methodology underlying staffing decisions is well documented.[51] *Standards for Internal Control in the Federal Government* also calls for clear documentation of policies and procedures that are readily available for examination.[52] These standards state that such control activities are an integral part of an entity's accountability for stewardship of government resources and achieving effective results. Without documented policies and procedures including its rationale and factors considered in allocating staff, OFO's staff allocation process lacks transparency and is therefore difficult for CBP officials or others to review and validate. As a result, CBP and its stakeholders do not have reasonable assurance that its staffing processes most effectively and efficiently allocate scarce resources to fulfill mission needs across ports.

CBP Performance Measures Do Not Reflect Progress in Achieving Trade Facilitation Goals

In fiscal year 2013, CBP identified 28 performance measures to assess and report on progress toward CBP's security and trade facilitation goals.[53] Nine measures were selected by DHS as Government Performance and Results Act (GPRA) measures (these are also called strategic measures within the department); 15 management measures are used to inform agency decisions on program priorities and resource allocation, and to monitor progress and performance; and 4 operational measures are maintained by OFO to capture former GPRA measures that

---

[51]See GAO-02-373SP.

[52]See GAO/AIMD-00-21.3.1.

[53]As mentioned previously, the agency's trade facilitation goals are articulated in DHS's February 2010 *Quadrennial Homeland Security Review Report,* which outlined a strategic framework for homeland security. DHS's two goals related to trade facilitation are (1) prevent the illegal flow of people and goods across U.S. air, land, and sea borders while expediting the safe flow of lawful travel and commerce, and (2) ensure security and resilience of global movement systems. See DHS, *Quadrennial Homeland Security Review Report: A Strategic Framework for a Secure Homeland.*

OFO continues to use internally.[54] (See appendix IV for a list of CBP's fiscal year 2013 performance measures.)

Two of these 28 performance measures address the level of participation in CBP's trade facilitation programs but none gauge the impact of CBP's trade facilitation efforts. Of the 28 measures, 26 are focused on security, enforcement, and compliance with trade laws, and 2 are focused on the agency's trade facilitation goals. These 2 measures include (1) *the percent of cargo by value imported to the United States by participants in CBP trade partnership programs*, and (2) *the percent increase in travelers to the United States enrolled in a Trusted Traveler program.*[55] These 2 measures can serve as indicators of the level of participation in CBP trade facilitation programs, such as FAST, and thus are important for CBP to track, but they do not provide information on whether these programs are facilitating trade because they do not measure desired outcomes for the programs.[56] OMB defines outcome as an event or condition that is of direct importance to the intended beneficiaries or the public, such as facilitated trade.[57] DHS's *Quadrennial Homeland Security Review Report*

---

[54]Pub. L. No. 103-62, 107 Stat. 285 (1993). GPRA seeks to improve the management of federal programs, as well as their effectiveness and efficiency, by establishing a system under which agencies set goals for program performance and measure their results. Specifically, GPRA requires executive agencies to prepare multiyear strategic plans, annual performance plans, and annual performance reports. The GPRA Modernization Act of 2010, Pub. L. No. 111-352, 124 Stat. 3866 (2011), amended GPRA to establish a framework aimed at taking a more crosscutting and integrated approach to focusing on results and improving government performance. Under this framework, organizational components of agencies, such as CBP, are not treated separately; rather, agencies are to work with their components to identify priorities, goals, and performance indicators relative to the mission and strategic objectives of the agency. See OMB Circular No. A-11, Section 200.1 (2012). In fiscal year 2013, DHS has designated 84 GPRA performance measures—9 of which focus on CBP efforts.

[55]*The percent of cargo by value imported to the United States by participants in CBP trade partnership programs* is a GPRA or strategic measure, and *the percent increase in travelers to the United States enrolled in a Trusted Traveler program* is a CBP operational measure. CBP's Trusted Traveler programs provide expedited travel for preapproved, low-risk travelers through dedicated lanes and kiosks. FAST is one of several such programs.

[56]According to CBP, the intended benefits to participants in the FAST trade partnership program include (1) access to dedicated lanes for greater speed and efficiency in processing transborder shipments; (2) reduced number of inspections resulting in reduced delays at the border; (3) priority, front-of-the-line processing for CBP inspections; and (4) enhanced supply chain security while promoting the economic prosperity of the United States, Canada, and Mexico.

[57]This definition of outcome comes from OMB Circular No. A-11, *Preparation, Submission, and Execution of the Budget* (Washington, D.C.: June 26, 2008).

stated that DHS would improve measurement of desired mission outcomes and the contribution of programs, activities, and resources to them. OFO and OA officials stated that CBP's existing performance measures imply that trade will be facilitated through increased participation in trade partnership programs rather than by directly measuring the desired outcomes. More specifically, OFO and OA officials stated that the measure *percent of cargo by value imported to the United States by participants in CBP trade partnership programs* implies that trade will be facilitated through participation in the programs, rather than directly measuring the desired outcomes of shorter wait times, for example. Similarly, OFO and OA officials told us that the measure *percent increase in travelers to the United States enrolled in a Trusted Traveler program* is not intended to capture the benefits to the program participants or trade facilitation, but, rather, is primarily an internal program measure that captures progress toward CBP's goal of growing enrollment in Trusted Traveler programs, including FAST.

DHS and CBP officials stated that they have not developed more performance measures for trade facilitation primarily because key stakeholders, including DHS leadership and Congress, have not pushed for this, and trade facilitation measures are difficult to develop. DHS and CBP officials reported that they have more performance measures focused on security and enforcement because these have been more of a focus for stakeholders than trade facilitation. In addition, CBP officials report that they have not created outcome-oriented measures for trade facilitation because the results of their trade facilitation efforts are difficult to capture in one or two measures. OFO and OA officials told us that it can be hard to articulate trade facilitation to external stakeholders because trade facilitation means different things to different stakeholders, each with its own interests. However, these same concerns could apply to outcome-oriented measures for CBP's security and enforcement efforts, and CBP has developed an outcome-oriented measure in that area—the land border interdiction rate for major violations. OFO and OA officials told us that this measure is the single best outcome measure for security, though they note that it is limited to passenger vehicles.[58] In addition, OMB guidance states that proxy measures that are closely tied to the desired outcome can be used to indirectly measure program outcomes

---

[58]OFO and OA officials explained that there is no such measure for commercial vehicles because the commercial environment is much more complex with more layers of review and the threshold that triggers an examination is much lower in the commercial setting.

when programs are difficult to measure because data are not available.[59] Potential outcome-oriented measures or proxy measures for trade facilitation could include, for example, measures to determine the extent to which CBP trusted shipper programs have met their goal, such as the percentage of time FAST traffic waits a certain percentage less time than regular commercial traffic or the ratio of FAST to non-FAST referrals to secondary inspection.

In the absence of outcome-oriented or proxy measures, CBP's ability to identify and publicly report the impact of the agency's trade facilitation programs is limited. OFO and OA officials reported that as a result of not having more outcome-oriented measures for trade facilitation, the agency is less prepared to identify and report the positive impact of its trade facilitation efforts to the public, and industry representatives we met with noted a lack of information on the impact of CBP's trade facilitation efforts. CBP officials at headquarters and in the field have stated that participation in the FAST program has resulted in shorter wait times for program participants, but Border Trade Alliance officials and industry representatives at two of the roundtables we held raised concerns that FAST program participants were not receiving these benefits and were unclear about the impact of this particular trade facilitation program.

OMB and our guidance recommend the use of outcome-oriented performance measures to promote accountability for results. Our guidance states that leading organizations promote accountability by establishing results-oriented outcome goals and corresponding measures by which to gauge progress.[60] This guidance further states that measuring performance allows organizations to track the progress they are making toward their goals and gives managers critical information on which to base decisions for improving their progress. More specifically, we identified establishing performance goals and measures to better translate activities into results as a useful practice to enhance performance management and measurement processes, and we have previously issued guidance that agencies should identify and use

---

[59]Office of Management and Budget, *Performance Measurement Challenges and Strategies*, (Washington, D.C.: June 18, 2003).

[60]See, for example, GAO, *Executive Guide: Effectively Implementing the Government Performance and Results Act*, GAO/GGD-96-118 (Washington, D.C.: June 1996).

outcome goals wherever possible to reflect the results of their activities.[61] In addition, OMB guidance encourages the use of outcome measures because they are much more meaningful to the public.[62] In the absence of meaningful outcome-oriented performance measures, or proxy measures, for trade facilitation—such as measures capturing whether FAST participants are receiving their intended benefits of quicker processing time and fewer inspections—it is difficult for CBP, decision makers, and other stakeholders to gauge CBP progress in achieving the agency's stated trade facilitation goals.

Conclusions

Trade between Mexico and the United States is important to the United States' economic health, and the value of goods imported into the U.S. from Mexico is on the rise. The length of time commercial vehicles wait in line at the border affects this trade activity. However, CBP's current wait time data are unreliable, limiting the extent to which CBP can use wait time data across border crossings to inform management decisions about infrastructure investment and staffing allocation and industry stakeholders can rely on publicly reported data. Taking steps to help CBP port officials implement CBP's existing mechanisms for collecting wait time data, consistent with agency guidance, could improve data reliability and usefulness for these purposes. Moreover, assessing the feasibility of options for automating wait time data consistent with program management standards could help CBP consider ways to reduce port officials' current burden in manually collecting the data and provide CBP with more reliable and comprehensive data it can use to identify and address challenges to trade facilitation.

---

[61]See GAO, *Managing for Results: Strengthening Regulatory Agencies' Performance Management Practices*, GAO/GGD-00-10 (Washington, D.C.: Oct. 28, 1999). In this report we gathered information from 23 federal and state organizations that we or other credible sources identified as using or planning to use a variety of useful practices to enhance specific aspects of their performance management and measurement processes. The organizations, although they had different missions, sizes, and organizational structures, said they consistently recognized that these practices are important in their efforts to develop a stronger results orientation. See also *The Results Act: An Evaluator's Guide to Assessing Agency Annual Performance Plans*, (GAO, GGD.10.1.20 (Washington, D.C.: April 1998).

[62]See OMB Circular No. A-11, *Preparation, Submission, and Execution of the Budget* (Washington, D.C.: Aug. 3, 2012). See also OMB, *Performance Measurement Challenges and Strategies* (Washington, D.C.: June 18, 2003).

CBP's ability to meet its mission goals—including both security and trade facilitation—are affected by its allocation of staff across the southwest border, among other things. In the absence of transparency about the methodology and process by which CBP allocates staff resources across ports of entry, it is difficult for CBP and others to evaluate whether existing staff have been allocated to most effectively address CBP's mission needs. Documenting CBP's staff allocation methodology in accordance with best practices for strategic workforce planning could help better position CBP to ensure that it is allocating its staff efficiently and effectively across ports of entry and border crossings.

In addition, it is difficult for CBP or others to gauge the agency's progress in meeting its trade facilitation goal because CBP does not have outcome-oriented measures for its trade facilitation efforts. Developing outcome-oriented, or proxy, performance measures that capture the impact of CBP's trade facilitation efforts, consistent with OMB and our guidance, could help CBP officials, Congress, and other stakeholders better assess the effectiveness of CBP's trade facilitation programs in supporting the agency's overall mission and goals.

Recommendations for Executive Action

We recommend that the Commissioner of CBP take four actions.

To improve the usefulness of southwest border crossing wait time data for informing public and management decisions, the Commissioner of CBP should take the following two actions:

- Identify and carry out steps that can be taken to help CBP port officials overcome challenges to consistent implementation of existing wait time estimation methodologies. Steps for ensuring consistent implementation of these methodologies could include, for example, implementing the fiscal year 2008 WHTI report recommendations to use closed-circuit television cameras to measure wait time in real time and provide a standardized measurement and validation tool.

- In consultation with FHWA and state DOTs, assess the feasibility of replacing current methods of manually calculating wait times with automated methods, which could include assessing all of the associated costs and benefits, options for how the agency will use and publicly report the results of automated data collection, the potential trade-offs associated with moving to this new system, and other factors such as those influencing the possible expansion of existing automation efforts to the 34 other locations that currently report wait times but have no automation projects under way.

To better ensure that CBP's OFO's staffing processes are transparent and to help ensure CBP can demonstrate that these resource decisions have effectively addressed CBP's mission needs, we recommend that the Commissioner of CBP document the methodology and process OFO uses to allocate staff to land ports of entry on the southwest border, including the rationales and factors considered in making these decisions.

To facilitate transparency and performance accountability for its trade facilitation programs and meeting CBP's goal of balancing its trade and security missions, we recommend that the Commissioner of CBP develop outcome-oriented performance measures or proxy measures to capture the impact of CBP's trade facilitation efforts, such as measures to determine the extent to which CBP trusted shipper programs have met their goals.

Agency Comments and Our Evaluation

We provided a draft of this report to DHS, GSA, DOT, the Department of Commerce, and the Department of Health and Human Services for their review and comment. GSA, DOT, the Department of Commerce, and Department of Health and Human Services did not have any comments on the draft of the report. DHS provided written comments, which are summarized below and reproduced in full in appendix VII. In the written comments, DHS concurred with our four recommendations and discussed actions to address them. However, the actions DHS identified will not address the intent of one of these recommendations. DHS also provided technical comments, which we incorporated, as appropriate.

DHS agreed with our first recommendation that CBP identify and carry out steps to help CBP port officials overcome challenges to consistent implementation of existing wait time estimation methodologies. In written comments, DHS officials explained that if funding is available, CBP has a goal to automate the estimation and reporting of border wait times. To this end, they plan to establish an internal and external stakeholder group and identify the best candidate technologies to pilot. These steps will help further CBP's longer-term plans to automate wait time data collection, but do not address the intent of our recommendation that CBP take steps to help port officials more consistently implement existing manual wait time estimation methodologies.

DHS agreed with our second recommendation that CBP assess the feasibility of replacing current methods of manually calculating wait times with automated methods. In commenting on a draft of this report, DHS officials noted that CBP has taken some steps to assess options for automating wait time data collection at northern and southern land border crossings and provided us with supplemental documents that included rough cost estimates for piloting, deploying, and maintaining automation technology. Based on this information, DHS requested that we consider this recommendation closed. While DHS has taken positive initial steps to address this recommendation, DHS should complete additional feasibility analysis to fully address the intent of our recommendation and better position the agency to decide whether and how to automate data collection. For example, DHS written comments stated that the feasibility of financing, funding, and operating automation technology is "reduced." More detailed and comprehensive cost analysis—such as estimating and comparing the costs of different technology solutions and analyzing potential funding sources—could help CBP assess the feasibility of wait time automation. In addition, DHS officials noted in their written comments that CBP has not yet identified the best technologies to pilot. Determining the best technology, if any, for use at each border crossing could influence the overall feasibility of planned automation across southwest border land ports of entry.

With regard to our third recommendation that CBP document the methodology and process OFO uses to allocate staff to land ports of entry, DHS agreed and stated that CBP will develop and document a standardized process for allocating CBP officers that includes assumptions, factors, and concerns to guide the decision-making process. If implemented effectively, these actions should meet the intent of our recommendation.

With regard to our fourth recommendation that CBP develop outcome-oriented performance measures or proxy measures to capture the impact of CBP's trade facilitation efforts, DHS concurred and stated that they plan to create a team of subject matter experts from OFO trade-related programs to identify at least two outcome measures or acceptable proxy measures for trade facilitation. They also noted plans to collaborate with private sector entities in order to identify metrics of greatest concern. If implemented effectively, these actions should meet the intent of our recommendation.

We are sending copies of this report to the Departments of Homeland Security, Commerce, Transportation, and Health and Human Services;

and the General Services Administration. The report is also available at no charge on the GAO website at http://www.gao.gov.

If you or your staff have any questions about this report, please contact me at (202) 512-8777, or at GamblerR@gao.gov. Contact points for our Office of Congressional Relations and Public Affairs may be found on the last page of this report. GAO staff who made major contributions to this report are listed in appendix VIII.

Sincerely yours,

Rebecca Gambler
Director
Homeland Security and Justice Issues

Appendix I: Results of Studies on the Economic Impact of Wait Times on Cross-Border Commerce

To determine what is known about the economic impact of wait time on cross-border commerce, we identified and analyzed relevant studies.[1] We searched academic, government, and other literature published from January 1, 2000, to June 30, 2012, to capture a wide array of recently published literature, and asked all relevant interviewees—including officials with the Department of Homeland Security's (DHS) U.S. Customs and Border Protection (CBP), Department of Commerce, trade associations, private industry, and academics—whether they were aware of any such studies.[2] We reviewed over 100 identified studies and narrowed our focus to the 6 studies that determined an economic impact of commercial vehicle wait times on the southwest border. We interviewed officials at the organizations that sponsored each of the qualifying studies to better understand the methodologies and limitations. We then analyzed the studies by comparing their methodologies with best practices for economic impact studies, including cost-benefit criteria in Office of Management and the Budget (OMB) Circular A-94 and comparing and contrasting the studies' scopes, methodologies, and findings.[3]

---

[1]Throughout this report, we use Customs and Border Protection's definition of wait time— the time it takes for a vehicle to travel from the end of the queue to the primary inspection point in the United States.

[2]We conducted both subject and key word literature searches utilizing more than 20 subject-specific bibliographic databases to systematically scan and identify academic, government, and other sources. Other sources scanned include gray literature—informally published written material—and government sources. We searched all sources for scholarly and peer-reviewed material, government reports, trade and industry articles, association and think tank publications, and working papers. As with any such literature search, there are a number of limitations to consider. This scan is a sample and does not attempt to review all published or gray literature on this topic. Attempting to scan all published and gray literature would be an immense task, and searching bibliographic databases represents a transparent and well-documented proxy for what is being expressed across the broader subject community. We recognize that there is a lag time in ideas and research findings making their way into the indexing of bibliographic databases as well as a growing amount of peer-reviewed material being retracted.

[3]OMB Circular A-94 Revised, *Guidelines and Discount Rates for Benefit-Cost Analysis of Federal Programs* (Washington, D.C.: Oct. 29, 1992).

Appendix I: Results of Studies on the
Economic Impact of Wait Times on Cross-
Border Commerce

CBP Study Estimated the Effect of Additional Staff at Ports of Entry on Wait Times and the U.S. Economy

An April 2013 CBP-commissioned study found that reduced waits at select border crossings would result in benefits to the U.S. economy in terms of increased gross domestic product (GDP) and jobs.[4] This study, conducted by the National Center for Risk and Economic Analysis of Terrorism, estimates the benefit of adding one CBP officer to select border land and air border crossings—assuming these added staff would each open one additional primary inspection lane—in terms of reduced waits and resulting benefits to the U.S. economy. The study found, for example, that at seven of the biggest southwest border commercial vehicle crossings, having one additional staff member open one additional primary inspection lane during the 8 most congested hours of the day would result in wait time reductions ranging from 1.5 minutes to 7.2 minutes for commercial vehicle traffic during those hours. The study then estimated that over the course of a year, these wait time reductions for commercial vehicles at these seven crossings would lead to direct economic benefits of $915,000 in GDP (in 2011 dollars) and 9.3 additional jobs.[5] CBP officials report that they plan to use the results of this study to demonstrate the benefit of adding CBP officers. These officials report that CBP has typically demonstrated its benefit in terms of number of seizures and arrests, for example, but this study will permit CBP to show an officer's trickledown effect on the U.S. economy.

However, we identified three limitations to consider regarding the reported economic benefits. First, this study estimated the benefits of this change but not the costs. CBP officials state that the study was not intended to be a cost-benefit analysis and noted that the types of costs that would have

---

[4]National Center for Risk and Economic Analysis of Terrorism Events, *The Impact on the U.S. Economy of Changes in Wait Times at Port of Entry*, April 4, 2013, a report prepared for DHS. The National Center for Risk and Economic Analysis of Terrorism Events is a university-based center of excellence funded by the Office of University Programs of the Science and Technology Directorate of DHS. The Center's mission is to improve U.S. security through research and development of models and tools to evaluate risks, costs, and consequences of terrorism and natural and manmade hazards, and to guide economically viable investments in homeland security.

[5]For the six commercial vehicle crossings we visited in the course of our study—Bridge of the Americas and Ysleta in El Paso, Texas; World Trade Bridge and Columbia Solidarity Bridge in Laredo, Texas; Mariposa in Nogales, Arizona; and Otay Mesa near San Diego, California—CBP's study found that having one additional staff member open one additional primary inspection lane during the 8 most congested hours of the day would result in wait time reductions ranging from 1.5 minutes to 6.3 minutes and would lead to direct economic benefits of $645,000 in GDP (in 2011 dollars) and 6.5 additional jobs. The estimated number of jobs created does not include the CBP officers added.

Appendix I: Results of Studies on the
Economic Impact of Wait Times on Cross-
Border Commerce

to be considered in a cost-benefit analysis include staff salaries, inspection booth and lane maintenance, and equipment. Second, the study assumes that one additional primary processing lane is available to be opened during the busiest 8 hours of the day. However, CBP officials report that at some crossings they already open all primary inspection lanes during peak hours. Therefore, this assumption is unrealistic or would require CBP investment in additional primary inspection lanes. Third, the study used CBP's reported wait time data for fiscal year 2012, which, as described earlier in this report, we determined are not sufficiently reliable for analysis across crossings, among other things.[6] Officials who conducted this study told us that they did not test the reliability of CBP's wait time data but found the basic data pattern plausible and therefore determined that the data were sufficiently reliable for their analysis.

Other Commissioned Studies Reported That Wait Times Directly Affect the U.S. Economy, Resulting in Lost Revenue and Jobs

Five other studies, one of which was commissioned by DHS, have quantified the effects of commercial vehicle wait times on cross-border commerce and also found evidence of lost revenue and jobs. The studies' findings are not comparable because of their differing scopes and methodologies, but they estimate direct impacts ranging from $452 million in the San Diego area to $1.9 billion across five cities with major border crossings. All five studies have limitations that may have led to an overstatement of the economic impacts of wait times. In particular, four of these studies used economic multipliers to quantify the effect of wait time delays on the U.S. economy. As stated in OMB Circular A-94, these secondary effects should not be used when measuring social benefits or costs. Rather, the reported effects should be limited to direct effects only. Therefore, we included only the direct impacts in our summary of these studies. The five studies' findings and limitations are summarized in table 2.

---

[6]CBP staff at each crossing manually collect and report hourly wait time data into CBP's Border Wait Time Administrative Tool.

Appendix I: Results of Studies on the
Economic Impact of Wait Times on Cross-
Border Commerce

Table 2: Studies of the Economic Impact of Commercial Vehicle Wait Times on the Southwest Border

Study name	Economic Impacts of Wait Times at the San Diego-Baja California Border, Final Report[a]	Improving Economic Outcomes by Reducing Border Delays: Facilitating the Vital Flow of Commercial Traffic Across the U.S.-Mexico Border[b]	Goods Movement Border Crossing Study and Analysis[c]	Economic Benefits of Expanding the Border-Crossing for Commercial Vehicles at the Mariposa Crossing in Nogales, Arizona[d]	El Paso Regional Ports of Entry Operations Plan[e]
Date published	January 19, 2006	Never officially published, but March 2008 version released	June 6, 2012	June 2007	June 2011
Commissioned by	San Diego Association of Governments California Department of Transportation, District 11	Department of Commerce's International Trade Administration	Southern California Association of Governments	U.S. Department of Homeland Security, Private Sector Office	Texas Department of Transportation
Commercial vehicle border crossings included in study	Otay Mesa and Tecate crossings at the border of San Diego County and the Mexican state of Baja California	Crossings at: • Laredo, Texas (World Trade Bridge and Columbia Solidarity Bridge) • El Paso, Texas (Bridge of the Americas and Ysleta) • San Diego, California (Otay Mesa) • Hidalgo, Texas (Pharr Reynosa International Bridge) • Nogales, Arizona (Mariposa)	Calexico East in Imperial County, California	Mariposa Crossing in Nogales, Arizona	Bridge of the Americas and Ysleta in El Paso, Texas and Santa Teresa in Santa Teresa, New Mexico

Appendix I: Results of Studies on the
Economic Impact of Wait Times on Cross-
Border Commerce

Study name	Economic Impacts of Wait Times at the San Diego-Baja California Border, Final Report[a]	Improving Economic Outcomes by Reducing Border Delays: Facilitating the Vital Flow of Commercial Traffic Across the U.S.-Mexico Border[b]	Goods Movement Border Crossing Study and Analysis[c]	Economic Benefits of Expanding the Border-Crossing for Commercial Vehicles at the Mariposa Crossing in Nogales, Arizona[d]	El Paso Regional Ports of Entry Operations Plan[e]
Period studied	2005	2008	2011	2003-2006	2010-2035 (period forecast)
Wait time data used	A sample of Otay Mesa wait time data collected by Batelle for the Department of Transportation's Federal Highway Administration in July 2001[f]	Original wait time data collected using high-resolution cameras.[g] CBP's historical wait time data were used to annualize and extrapolate the observed wait times[h] Total wait time was defined as the time elapsed from entering the line in Mexico leading to Mexican inspection through exit from U.S. inspection facilities, including any U.S. state-conducted inspections. The authors note that this represents an expanded definition of wait time.	Original wait time data collected using high-resolution cameras.[g]	CBP's historical wait time data[h] supplemented with interviews with local businesses and a field study of wait times and traffic flows at Mariposa.	CBP wait time data for April 24, 2010, was modeled and forecast through 2035.
Findings of direct effects	In 2005, delays in freight movement resulted in a total direct loss of $452 million in output, $99 million in labor income losses, and 2,117 jobs lost.	In 2008, commercial vehicle wait times at these five crossings resulted in $1.9 billion in direct economic loss, 4,939 jobs, and a labor income loss of $322 million.	In 2011, delays in both northbound and southbound commercial vehicle traffic at the Calexico East border crossing resulted in economic losses of $49 million and 334 jobs in Imperial County, California, and losses of $98 million and 1,000 jobs in the state of California.	A 50 percent reduction in wait time for commercial vehicles is expected to result in a direct increase in output of $2.9 million and create 25 jobs per year.	In 2010 the regional economy lost $90 million and 2,551 jobs. Assuming no changes in current infrastructure or operations (no-build scenario), by 2035, waits are estimated to reach 11 hours, which would contract the regional economy by $54 billion and cause a net loss of 857,000 jobs.

Appendix I: Results of Studies on the
Economic Impact of Wait Times on Cross-
Border Commerce

Study name	Economic Impacts of Wait Times at the San Diego-Baja California Border, Final Report[a]	Improving Economic Outcomes by Reducing Border Delays: Facilitating the Vital Flow of Commercial Traffic Across the U.S.-Mexico Border[b]	Goods Movement Border Crossing Study and Analysis[c]	Economic Benefits of Expanding the Border-Crossing for Commercial Vehicles at the Mariposa Crossing in Nogales, Arizona[d]	El Paso Regional Ports of Entry Operations Plan[e]
Study limitations	Model included multiplier effects which, per the Office of Management and Budget's Circular A-94, should not be included in the cost-benefit analysis. Therefore, we included only the direct effects in our summary. Model calculates the economic impact of the full length of the wait time, implying that the alternative is a wait of zero minutes. This alternative is an implausible scenario since some wait time and associated economic loss will always exist. It is not clear what the optimal level of wait time is, but if the optimal wait time were 20 minutes, for example, then economic losses should be estimated based on the difference between the estimated wait time and 20 minutes rather than on the full wait time.			Model included multiplier effects that, per the Office of Management and Budget's Circular A-94, should not be included in the cost-benefit analysis. Therefore, we included only the direct effects in our summary.	For 2010, the model calculates the economic impact of the full length of the wait time, implying that the alternative is a wait of zero minutes. This alternative is an implausible scenario since some wait time and associated economic loss will always exist. It is not clear what the optimal level of wait time is, but if the optimal wait time were 20 minutes, for example, then economic losses should be estimated based on the difference between the estimated wait time and 20 minutes rather than on the full wait time. The economic impact for the period 2011 through 2035 is calculated using the 2010 wait time as a baseline. Study uses CBP data that we found not reliable for the purposes of this study.[h] Study calibrates wait time data based on 1 day of high traffic volume.

Appendix I: Results of Studies on the
Economic Impact of Wait Times on Cross-
Border Commerce

Study name	Economic Impacts of Wait Times at the San Diego-Baja California Border, Final Report[a]	Improving Economic Outcomes by Reducing Border Delays: Facilitating the Vital Flow of Commercial Traffic Across the U.S.-Mexico Border[b]	Goods Movement Border Crossing Study and Analysis[c]	Economic Benefits of Expanding the Border-Crossing for Commercial Vehicles at the Mariposa Crossing in Nogales, Arizona[d]	El Paso Regional Ports of Entry Operations Plan[e]
					Forecast 11-hour wait in 2035 does not take into account travelers' sensitivity to wait time with respect to the value or purpose of their trip.

Source: GAO analysis of published studies.

[a]HDR/HLB Decision Economics Inc., *Economic Impacts of Wait Times at the San Diego-Baja California Border, Final Report*, a report prepared at the request of the San Diego Association of Governments and California Department of Transportation, District 11, January 19, 2006.

[b]Accenture, *Improving Economic Outcomes by Reducing Border Delays: Facilitating the Vital Flow of Commercial Traffic across the U.S.-Mexico Border* (Draft), a study prepared for the Department of Commerce's International Trade, March 2008. Department of Commerce officials told us that the study was not given interagency clearance so was not published but, rather, was made public in response to a subsequent Freedom of Information Act request.

[c]HDR Decision Economics, *Goods Movement Border Crossing Study and Analysis* (Final Report), a report prepared for the Southern California Association of Government, June 6, 2012.

[d]RTI International, *Economic Benefits of Expanding the Border-Crossing for Commercial Vehicles at the Mariposa Crossing in Nogales, Arizona* (Final Report), a report prepared for the U.S. Department of Homeland Security, Private Sector Office, June 2007.

[e]Cambridge Systematics, Inc., *El Paso Regional Ports of Entry Operations Plan* (Final Report), a report prepared for the Texas Department of Transportation, June 2011.

[f]Battelle is a nonprofit research and development organization that focuses on science and technology research for the national security, health and life sciences, and energy and environmental industries. The wait time data it collected for the Department of Transportation's Federal Highway Administration are referenced in *Evaluation of Travel Time Methods to Support Mobility Performance Monitoring* –Otay Mesa, Office of Freight Management and Operations, Federal Highway Administration, April 2002.

[g]High-resolution cameras were used to record photographs of the trucks' license plates at various points along the crossing route. These photographs were then matched to identify crossing times per vehicle.

[h]As described previously in this report, we reviewed CBP's wait time data and determined that the data were not reliable for some purposes such as comparison across border crossings.

Appendix II: Objectives, Scope, and Methodology

This report addresses the following questions:

- To what extent are CBP wait time data reliable for public reporting and informing CBP decisions on staffing and infrastructure investments?

- To what extent has CBP identified infrastructure and staffing needed to process current commercial traffic volume at southwest border crossings with high traffic volume?

- To what extent do CBP performance measures address progress toward its goal of facilitating trade?

This report also presents information on the results of studies that have quantified the economic impact of commercial vehicle wait times on cross-border commerce. This information, including the methodology used to identify these studies, is presented in appendix I.

To inform our analysis of the first and second objectives, we visited six crossings at four land ports of entry: Bridge of the Americas and Ysleta at El Paso, Texas; World Trade Bridge and Columbia Solidarity Bridge at Laredo, Texas; Mariposa at Nogales, Arizona; and Otay Mesa near San Diego, California. We selected these crossings based on their commercial traffic volume, and geographic diversity, and to include representation of crossings with a mix of recent or ongoing infrastructure modernization projects. At each location, we interviewed CBP management, toured the facility, and convened a roundtable of local industry representatives and local government officials. To obtain a range of perspectives on commercial vehicle traffic at southwest border crossings, we met with representatives of 21 companies and associations (who were identified to us as knowledgeable stakeholders) representing industries that rely on cross-border commerce including customs brokers, trucking companies, and distributors), as well as bridge directors and representatives of four local government entities (the Mayors of El Paso and San Diego, the Laredo City Manager, and representatives of the San Diego Association of Governments) at all four cities we visited or by teleconference.[1] Because we focused on four land ports of entry with six commercial vehicle crossings, our findings are not generalizable to the entire southwest border. However, the ports we visited accounted for, in total,

---

[1]The San Diego Association of Governments is a public planning, transportation, transit construction, and research agency.

approximately 70 percent of the commercial vehicle crossings into the
United States from Mexico in fiscal years 2008 through July 2012. Over
the course of our work, we also interviewed officials from agencies
involved in securing the border and facilitating trade at land ports of entry,
including officials from CBP's Office of Administration and Office of Field
Operations, the General Services Administration (GSA), the Department
of Transportation's (DOT) Federal Highway Administration and Federal
Motor Carrier Safety Administration, the Department of Commerce
(Commerce), the Department of Health and Human Service's Food and
Drug Administration, and the Department of State. We also interviewed
other stakeholders, including officials from the Mexican Foreign Ministry,
academics, and representatives of national trade associations, including
the American Trucking Associations and the Border Trade Alliance, to
obtain a broader range of perspectives on commercial vehicle traffic at
southwest border crossings.[2]

To address the first objective, we reviewed and analyzed CBP's policies
and guidance for calculating and reporting wait times to determine the
source of these data and the agency's control over these data. We
interviewed CBP headquarters officials about the wait time data, including
data quality, data entry protocols, quality assurance procedures, and any
steps taken to improve the reliability of these data. We also interviewed
officials at the six crossings we visited about how they collect and report
wait time data. We reviewed CBP documents evaluating the quality of
CBP's wait time data on the southwest border, including a fiscal year
2008 CBP *Commercial Wait Times Analysis Report*.[3] We compared
documentary and testimonial evidence of how wait times are currently
being calculated by officials at land ports of entry on the southwest border

---

[2]These organizations and officials were identified to us as knowledgeable stakeholders
who could provide us with a range of perspectives on commercial vehicle traffic at
southwest border crossings. The American Trucking Associations is a national trade and
safety organization representing the U.S. trucking industry. The Border Trade Alliance is a
nonprofit organization that serves as a forum for participants to address key issues
affecting trade, travel, and security in North America.

[3]CBP reported on the reliability of wait time calculations in its *Western Hemisphere Travel
Initiative (WHTI), Commercial Wait Times Analysis Final Report, October 2007 –
September 2008*. The goal of WHTI is to facilitate entry for U.S. citizens and legitimate
foreign visitors while strengthening U.S. border security. The WHTI Program Office
sponsored this evaluation of commercial vehicle wait times to validate the current wait
time reporting systems at individual crossings and to determine if a national standard for
reporting wait times can be established.

against CBP policies and guidance to identify any discrepancies. We reviewed CBP's data and reports on wait times for the six crossings for fiscal year 2012. In addition, to obtain non-CBP perspectives on CBP's methods for calculating wait times and the quality and usefulness of CBP's wait time data, we interviewed DOT officials, local officials, industry groups, and a Mexican official.[4] We compared CBP's policies and procedures for collecting and maintaining wait times data with criteria in *Standards for Internal Control in the Federal Government*.[5] According to the assessment, the usefulness of the wait time data is limited and the reliability of the data is not insufficient for certain purposes, such as for comparisons across ports. To determine how CBP officials use the agency's wait time data to inform management decisions, we analyzed CBP guidance, policy, and other documents as well as interviewed CBP officials from headquarters and the six crossings to determine the extent to which wait times are a factor in CBP staff allocation decisions and infrastructure investment requests and decisions. To determine the status of DOT's pilot projects to automate wait time data at the southwest border, we interviewed officials at DOT's Federal Highway Administration, Texas Department of Transportation, and Texas A&M University and reviewed documentary evidence they provided. We compared evidence of CBP's stated plans to automate wait times with criteria on standards for program management.[6]

To address the second objective, we reviewed and analyzed CBP and GSA assessments of land port of entry condition and capacity, such as CBP's Strategic Resource Assessments and GSA's BorderWizard™

---

[4]We selected these non-CBP stakeholders to provide us with a range of perspectives on commercial vehicle traffic at southwest border crossings. The results of these interviews are not generalizable but rather provide context for CBP officials' perspectives on these issues.

[5]GAO, *Standards for Internal Control in the Federal Government*, GAO/AIMD-00-21.3.1 (Washington, D.C.: November 1999). These standards, issued pursuant to the requirements of the Federal Managers' Financial Integrity Act of 1982, Pub. L. No. 97-255, 96 Stat. 814, provide the overall framework for establishing and maintaining internal control in the federal government.

[6]Project Management Institute, *The Standard for Program Management*©, Second Edition, (Newton Square, Pennsylvania: 2008).

reports.[7] We also interviewed CBP and GSA officials about infrastructure
needs at land border crossings and how these needs are identified and
prioritized. We reviewed documentation of CBP's workload staffing
model, which is used to determine staff needs at land ports of entry, and
interviewed CBP officials about the agency's staff allocation policies and
processes and compared these with criteria in our previous work on
human capital management and *Standards for Internal Control in the
Federal Government*.[8] In addition, we conducted an analysis of CBP's
hourly data on traffic volume and number of primary lanes open at the six
selected crossings to determine the extent to which CBP has utilized
primary lanes for commercial vehicle traffic from fiscal years 2008 through
2012. We selected this 5-year period to provide a sufficiently long time
period for trend analysis. As our analysis focused on identifying trends in
routine commercial vehicle traffic by crossing, we included both Free and
Secure Trade (FAST) and non-FAST traffic volume and lanes, but
excluded hazardous materials traffic.[9] To ensure data reliability, we did
not include any records on traffic volume or lanes open that fell outside
CBP's reported hours of operation. In addition, within the reported hours
of operation, we included the data in our analysis for any given hour if
CBP provided records for both traffic volume and lanes open. We
conducted this analysis for the six crossings we visited; thus our findings
are not generalizable to the entire southwest border. However, these six
crossings processed approximately 70 percent of commercial vehicle

---

[7]The strategic resource assessment is a needs assessment process by which CBP
collects and analyzes information about the infrastructure at each crossing, identifies
needs, and prioritizes infrastructure improvement projects along the northern and southern
borders. CBP officials reported conducting these assessments fiscal years 2003 through
2006. BorderWizard™ analyses serve as a decision-making resource/reference for GSA
and assist GSA in planning and designing land ports of entry.

[8]For prior work on human capital management see GAO, *A Model of Strategic Human
Capital Management,* GAO-02-373SP (Washington, D.C.: March 2002), and
GAO/AIMD-00-21.3.1. This report descr bes a human capital model we developed that
identifies eight critical success factors for managing human capital strategically. In
developing this model, we built upon GAO's *Human Capital: A Self-Assessment Checklist
for Agency Leaders* (GAO/OCG-00-14G, September 2000). Among other steps, we also
considered lessons learned from GAO reports on public and private organizations that are
viewed as leaders in strategic human capital management and managing for results. See
also GAO, *Standards for Internal Control in the Federal Government,*
GAO/AIMD-00-21.3.1

[9]CBP initiated the FAST program in 2002 to expedite the travel of low-risk screened
shipments across the border. Many land border crossings have dedicated FAST lanes to
expedite FAST traffic.

traffic coming into the United States from Mexico for fiscal year 2008 through July 2012. To assess the reliability of these data, we reviewed relevant documentation; interviewed knowledgeable agency officials; and electronically tested for missing data during hours of operation, outlier records outside of hours of operation, and obvious errors (such as data records showing traffic being processed when no lanes were reportedly open). We also reviewed related internal controls and traced a selection of data to source files. We determined that the data were sufficiently reliable for the purposes of our report.

In addition, to address the second objective, we asked CBP officials at headquarters, field offices, and ports of entry about (1) the sufficiency of staffing levels and infrastructure capacity to process the current volume of commercial traffic at the six crossings we visited, (2) CBP assessment and consideration of any staffing or infrastructure gaps when making resource allocation decisions, (3) CBP actions and plans to address any of these gaps, and (4) any challenges to effectively responding to any gaps that CBP identified. We also discussed CBP processes for determining staff needs at land ports of entry and allocating staff to the ports of entry. We then compared CBP's staffing policies and processes with criteria in our previous work on human capital management and *Standards for Internal Control in the Federal Government*.[10] In addition, we discussed CBP's workload staffing model and how it has been used to inform staffing processes with CBP officials responsible for the model. In addition, we interviewed relevant GSA, state, and local officials, as well as nongovernmental stakeholders regarding any coordinated efforts to identify, prioritize, and implement infrastructure improvements at land ports of entry on the southwest border.

To address the third objective, we reviewed documentation of CBP's fiscal year 2013 performance goals, measures, and reports. We then assessed CBP's measures against criteria in OMB Circular No. A-11 and useful practices GAO previously identified to enhance performance management and measurement processes to determine the extent to which CBP's existing performance measures capture progress toward

---

[10]See GAO-02-373SP and GAO/AIMD-00-21.3.1.

goals and incorporate successful practices.[11] We also interviewed
relevant DHS and CBP officials about CBP's current performance
measures, the adequacy of these measures, their perspectives on the
balance between the agency's security and trade facilitation goals, and
the extent to which CBP uses its wait time data to measure progress.

We also identified studies that quantified the economic impact of
commercial vehicle wait times on cross-border commerce by searching
literature and asking relevant interviewees whether they were aware of
any such studies. We reviewed over 100 identified studies and analyzed
the six studies that determined an economic impact of commercial vehicle
wait times on the southwest border. A more detailed description of our
methodology and the results of these studies are presented in appendix I.

We conducted this performance audit from July 2012 to July 2013 in
accordance with generally accepted government auditing standards.
Those standards require that we plan and perform the audit to obtain
sufficient, appropriate evidence to provide a reasonable basis for our
findings and conclusions based on our audit objectives. We believe that
the evidence obtained provides a reasonable basis for our findings and
conclusions based on our audit objectives.

---

[11]See OMB Circular No. A-11, *Preparation, Submission, and Execution of the Budget*
(Washington, D.C.: Aug. 3, 2012). See also GAO, *Managing for Results: Strengthening
Regulatory Agencies' Performance Management Practices*, GAO/GGD-00-10
(Washington, D.C.: Oct. 28, 1999). In this report we gathered information from 23 federal
and state organizations that we or other credible sources identified as using or planning to
use a variety of useful practices to enhance specific aspects of their performance
management and measurement processes. The organizations, although they had different
missions, sizes, and organizational structures, said they consistently recognized that
these practices are important in their efforts to develop a stronger results orientation.

Appendix III: U.S. Customs and Border Protection's Capital Investment Planning Process

This appendix describes CBP's reported process for identifying and prioritizing its infrastructure investment needs at land ports of entry on the northern and southwestern land borders.

According to CBP documents, CBP identifies and prioritizes the infrastructure needs of land ports of entry through a six-part process that culminates in a 5-year-plan.[1] The Department of Homeland Security Appropriations Act for fiscal year 2009 required beginning in fiscal year 2010 and every year thereafter, that CBP's annual budget submission for construction include, in consultation with GSA, a detailed 5-year plan for all federal land port of entry projects with a yearly update of total projected future funding needs.[2] This process, known as the capital investment plan (CIP), includes gathering data through Strategic Resource Assessments (SRA), scoring identified needs at each land port of entry using data and information gathered from the SRA, conducting a sensitivity analysis on the initial ranking of needs, assessing projects' feasibility and risk, using the information gathered from the previous steps in the process to develop and issue CBP's 5-year capital investment plan, and assessing the CIP process. Each step is described in further detail below.

1. **Strategic Resource Assessments**

   According to CBP, the first stage in the CIP is to conduct SRAs, which are infrastructure needs assessments intended to gather and present data to support the prioritization of CBP's facility projects on a national level. The SRA includes internal and external stakeholder input, workload and personnel forecasts, space capacity analyses, architectural evaluation of port facilities, and recommended options to meet current and future space needs.

---

[1]Department of Homeland Security, U.S. Customs and Border Protection, *Land Port of Entry Modernization: Promoting Security, Travel and Trade Fiscal Year 2012 Report to Congress*, (Washington, D.C.: June 2012).

[2]Pub. L. No. 110-329, div. D, 122 Stat. 3652, 3658 (2008). The fiscal year 2010 DHS appropriation included the same language. *See* Pub. L. No. 111-83, 123 Stat. 2142, 2148 (2009). In fiscal year 2012, the DHS appropriation included similar language but also required that the projected future funding needs be delineated by land port of entry. *See* Pub. L. No. 112-74, div. D., 125 Stat. 943, 949 (2011). The fiscal year 2011 continuing resolution and the fiscal year 2013 DHS appropriation did not include this language. *See* Pub. L. No. 112-10, 125 Stat. 38, 140; Pub. L. No. 113-6, div. D, 127 Stat. 342, 346.

2. Capital Project Scoring

Once CBP has completed the SRAs, the agency scores the
infrastructure needs of each land port of entry by the criticality of its
need for modernization using the data collected by the SRA. This
score is calculated by combining the data collected in the SRA with 60
distinct criteria within the predefined four categories (see table 3),
adjusted to reflect the relative weight of each category. For example,
factors CBP considers under the Personnel and Workload Growth
category include current and projected commercial vehicle traffic
volume as well as the current peak and projected number of
inspections personnel over the next 10-year period.

**Table 3: Categories of Criteria Customs and Border Protection Uses to Prioritize
Land Port of Entry Projects**

Category	Weight (by percent)
Mission and Operations	35
Security and Life Safety	25
Space and Site Deficiencies	25
Personnel and Workload Growth	15

Source: U.S. Customs and Border Protection.

Table 4 summarizes the priority rank assigned to the SRA-identified
infrastructure needs at land ports of entry on the southwest border that
process commercial vehicle traffic. The crossings are listed below in order
of their ranking relative to CBP's entire portfolio of land ports of entry on
northern and southwestern borders, including facilities that process bus,
commercial, passenger, pedestrian, and rail traffic.

**Table 4: Prioritization Rank of Infrastructure Needs at Commercial Southwest
Border Crossings**

Crossing and location	Overall rank
Tornillo: Fabens, Texas[a]	14
Bridge of the Americas: El Paso, Texas[b]	15
Roma, Texas	22
Douglas, Arizona	31
Mariposa: Nogales, Arizona[a, b]	34
Progreso, Texas	35
San Luis, Arizona[c]	48
Ysleta: El Paso, Texas[b, c]	53
Del Rio, Texas[c]	61

Crossing and location	Overall rank
Los Tomates: Brownsville, Texas	65
Columbus, New Mexico	66
Otay Mesa, California[b, c]	96
Presidio, Texas	102
World Trade Bridge: Laredo, Texas[b, c]	106
Naco, Arizona	109
Santa Teresa, New Mexico[a]	112
Lukeville, Arizona	116
Sasabe, Arizona	117
Eagle Pass Bridge II: Eagle Pass, Texas[d]	126
Pharr, Texas	129
Colombia Solidarity Bridge: Laredo, Texas[b]	132
Los Indios, Texas	134
Starr-Camargo Bridge: Rio Grande City, Texas	144
Tecate, California	150
Calexico East, California	151

Source: GAO analysis of CBP documents.

Notes: Each crossing's rank is relative to all crossings on both borders regardless of the type of traffic processed at the facility.

This list includes only ports of entry on the southwest border in existence at the time of CBP's completion of the SRA process: December 5, 2005. As a result, crossings built to address needs identified in the SRA, such as constructing San Luis II to address needs identified at San Luis, are not included on this list.

[a]Crossing where the General Services Administration (GSA) has an ongoing infrastructure project as of May 2013.

[b]Crossing we selected for site visit.

[c]Crossing where GSA completed an infrastructure project(s) in fiscal years 2008-2012.

[d]GSA plans to undertake an infrastructure project at Eagle Pass II in fiscal year 2013.

3. Sensitivity Analysis

CBP applies a sensitivity analysis of the initial ranking to determine if the results should consider factors unaccounted for through the standard SRA process, such as any unique regional conditions; bilateral planning and international partner interests; or interests of other U.S. federal, state, or local agencies. According to CBP officials, recent examples of factors CBP has considered include the identification of new manufacturing developments immediately adjacent to an existing land port of entry facility that would increase the demand for commercial processing capacities, facility damage resulting from floods that occurred after the SRA was completed in 2006, and the development of new land port of entry facility proposals in the same transportation region as an existing facility. CBP officials report that this information helps CBP identify additional drivers, constraints, and legislative mandates that may change the critical needs ranking.

4. **Risk and Feasibility Assessments**

In this phase, CBP coordinates with key project stakeholders such as GSA to evaluate the feasibility and risk associated with project implementation including environmental, cultural, and historic preservation requirements as well as land acquisition requirements. Additionally, according to senior CBP officials, CBP considers the likelihood of obtaining the necessary resources to fund the proposed project.

5. **5-Year Capital Investment Plan**

Once CBP has taken the previous steps, it uses the information and analyses to develop its capital investment plan, in coordination with GSA. CBP and GSA update the capital investment plan annually, taking into account any changes in DHS's mission and strategy, the changing conditions at land ports of entry, and any other factors discovered in the course of projects already under way. With each update, CBP identifies which projects are of highest priority. GSA then works with CBP to identify which projects may be considered for near-term design and construction funding, which require an initial or updated feasibility study, or which require further evaluation to account for issues such as environmental and local community concerns.

6. **Assessment of the CIP Methodology**

In response to expected budget constraints and as a general revalidation of its existing planning cycle, according to CBP Office of Administration officials and CBP documents, CBP is revisiting the process it uses to develop the 5-year plan. Although the assessment is in development, CBP aims to better incorporate up-front stakeholder involvement, place additional emphasis on state and local government-driven master planning fed by regional trend analyses, adopt a consistent and comprehensive communications approach, evaluate alternative funding mechanisms, assess broader programmatic needs, and target high-impact and lower-cost investments.

Appendix IV: Ongoing, Planned, or Completed Land Port of Entry Renovation Projects, Fiscal Years 2008 through 2012

The tables in this appendix summarize infrastructure improvement projects that CBP and GSA officials reported were completed from fiscal year 2008 through 2012 at southwest border land ports of entry that process commercial traffic as well as infrastructure improvement projects GSA and CBP reported to be ongoing or in planning or design phases as of May 2013.[1] GSA's Federal Buildings Fund included $564 million for land port of entry infrastructure improvement projects in fiscal years 2008 through 2010 and none in fiscal years 2011 and 2012. In addition, the American Recovery and Reinvestment Act (ARRA) of 2009 allocated $300 million for the GSA-owned land ports of entry that is being used to provide design or construction funds to seven new or ongoing capital projects.[2] CBP officials reported that the completed projects presented in table 4 cost a total of approximately $115 million and estimates that ongoing and planned projects to renovate these land ports of entry, presented in table 5, will cost approximately $370 million.

Table 5 summarizes the five infrastructure improvement projects GSA completed at southwest border land ports of entry that process commercial traffic in the period of fiscal years 2008 through 2012. Three of these projects were at crossings we visited—World Trade Bridge in Laredo, Texas; Ysleta in El Paso, Texas; and Otay Mesa near San Diego, California.

---

[1] We included projects completed or in development over the last 5 fiscal years to provide a perspective on the most recent projects completed or under way. We excluded small-scale projects, such as the addition of two exit booths at the Bridge of Americas in El Paso, Texas, in 2012, because these projects are primarily funded out of CBP's Office of Field Operation's operation budget—not GSA's Federal Building Fund or American Reconstruction and Recovery Act.

[2] Pub. L. No. 111-5, 123 Stat. 115, 149. Two of the seven GSA-owned land port of entry ARRA-funded projects were for crossings that process commercial traffic on the southwest border: Mariposa in Arizona, and Santa Teresa in New Mexico. The remainder of the funds were for crossings that are located on the northern border or do not process commercial traffic. In addition, ARRA also allocated another $420 million to modernize 31 existing land crossings owned by CBP. See 123 Stat. at 162. However, all but three of these projects were for crossings on the northern border, and none of the projects were for crossings on the southwest border that process commercial traffic.

Table 5: Completed Infrastructure Improvement Projects at Southwest Border Land Ports of Entry That Process Commercial Vehicle Traffic, Fiscal Years 2008 through 2012

Project title	Infrastructure improvement project description	Location	Sources (both federal and nonfederal) and amounts of funding provided for the project	Total project cost	Date of completion
Del Rio Land Port of Entry Modernization Project	This project was a complete port replacement and expansion.	Del Rio, Texas	GSA Federal Buildings Fund–$24 million, CBP Appropriations–$4.3 million	$28.3 million	June 2009
San Luis II Land Port of Entry Construction Project	This project constructed a new port, San Luis II. The project redirected commercial traffic from the San Luis I crossing to the new San Luis II crossing to improve commercial traffic flow and processing capacity.	San Luis II, Arizona	GSA Federal Buildings Fund–$42 million, CBP Appropriations–$7.6 million	$49.6 million	October 2010
Laredo III: World Trade Bridge Land Port of Entry Commercial Lane Expansion Project	The project added seven new commercial primary inspection lanes and a bypass lane to facilitate traffic flow and increase commercial processing capacity.	Laredo Bridge III: World Trade Bridge, Texas	City of Laredo funding-$7.5 million, GSA Repairs & Alterations Appropriations–$1.3 million, CBP Appropriations–$1.6 million	$10.4 million	April 2011
Ysleta Commercial Lane Expansion Project	The project added two commercial primary inspection lanes to increase processing capacity and reconfigured the site to create direct access to the Texas Department of Transportation safety inspection facility.	Ysleta, Texas	GSA Federal Buildings Fund–$20.2 million, CBP Appropriations–$3.6 million	$23.8 million	May 2009
Otay Mesa Land Port of Entry Commercial Lane Realignment Projects	The project improved the curvature of the existing commercial lanes and added Free and Secure Trade (FAST) technology to booths to facilitate traffic flow and increase commercial processing capacity, improved commercial traffic flow, and increased processing capacity.	Otay Mesa, California	California Department of Transportation–$2.6 million, CBP Appropriations–$0.5 million	$3.1 million	December 2009

Project title	Infrastructure improvement project description	Location	Sources (both federal and nonfederal) and amounts of funding provided for the project	Total project cost	Date of completion
Total all projects fiscal years 2008 through 2012			GSA appropriations: $87.5 million	$115.2 million	
			CBP appropriations: $17.6 million		
			Non-federal sources: $10.1 million		

Source: GAO analysis of GSA and CBP documents and officials' statements.

Table 6 summarizes the three ongoing GSA infrastructure improvement projects at southwest border land ports of entry that process commercial traffic as of May 2013.

Table 6: Ongoing Infrastructure Improvement Projects at Southwest Border Land Ports of Entry That Process Commercial Vehicle Traffic as of May 2013

Project title	Infrastructure improvement project description	Location (specific border crossing affected)	Sources (both federal and nonfederal) and amounts of funding to be provided for the project	Estimated total project cost	Expected date of completion
Tornillo-Guadalupe Land Port of Entry Modernization Project	The project is to replace and expand the existing facility including adding two commercial lanes capacity to the currently passenger-only port.	Tornillo: Guadalupe, Texas	GSA Federal Buildings Fund–$95.9 million, CBP Appropriations–$14.3 million	$79.6 million[a]	Summer 2013
Nogales West—Mariposa Land Port of Entry Modernization Project	This project is to replace and expand the existing facility, including major outbound infrastructure improvements and adding four commercial inspection lanes.	Nogales West: Mariposa, Arizona	GSA Federal Buildings Fund–$9.8 million (design), GSA ARRA–$182.7 million, CBP ARRA Savings–$10.5 million,[b] CBP Appropriations–$36.5 million	$239.5 million	Fall 2014
Santa Teresa Land Port of Entry Lane Expansion Project	This project is to expand the facility, including an additional commercial processing lane.	Santa Teresa, New Mexico	ARRA Savings–$10 million CBP Reimbursable Work Authorization–$1.3 million[c]	$11.3 million	February 2013

Project title	Infrastructure improvement project description	Location (specific border crossing affected)	Sources (both federal and nonfederal) and amounts of funding to be provided for the project	Estimated total project cost	Expected date of completion
Total fiscal years 2008 through 2012			GSA appropriations: $105.7 million ARRA: $203.2 million CBP appropriations: $50.8 million CBP Reimbursable Work Authorization: $1.3 million	$330.4 million	

Source: GAO analysis of GSA and CBP documents and officials' statements.

[a]According to GSA officials, Congress appropriated about $95.9 million for the Tornillo-Guadalupe project, and the total project cost is expected to be $79.6 million or less.

[b]These funds were derived from unused ARRA funds that were reprogrammed to other projects because of savings or changes to the original projects.

[c]Reimbursable Work Authorizations are established to capture and bill the costs of altering, repairing, renovating, or providing services in space managed by GSA, over and above the basic operations financed through rent.

Table 7 summarizes the one planned infrastructure improvement project at a southwest border land port of entry that processes commercial traffic.

Table 7: Planned Infrastructure Improvement Projects at Southwest Border Land Ports of Entry That Process Commercial Vehicle Traffic, as of May 2013

Project title	Infrastructure improvement project description	Location (specific border crossing affected)	Sources (both federal and nonfederal) and amounts of funding to be provided for the project	Estimated total project cost	Expected start date
Eagle Pass II Commercial Lane Realignment Project	The project is to improve the curvature of the two existing commercial lanes to facilitate traffic flow and increase commercial processing capacity.	Eagle Pass II, Texas	City of Eagle Pass–$6.6 million, CBP Repairs & Alterations budget–$0.4 million	$7 million	Summer to fall 2013
Project total			$7 million	$7 million	

Source: GAO analysis of GSA and CBP documents and officials' statements.

Appendix V: Average Hourly Traffic Volume and Average Hourly Percentage of Lanes Open Per Month, Fiscal Years 2008-2012

This appendix provides additional information on the average hourly traffic volume and average hourly percentage of lanes open per month at selected crossings, for fiscal years 2008 through 2012. Table 8 describes, for each of six selected land border crossings on the southwest border that process commercial vehicle traffic, (1) the year the crossing was built and last renovated, and (2) the number of primary inspection lanes for commercial vehicles in fiscal years 2008 through 2012. Figures 4 to 9 illustrate the layout of five of the six selected crossings and the primary inspection lanes of the remaining crossing for which CBP was not able to provide an aerial photo. Tables 8 through 13 provide the average hourly traffic volume, per month and the average hourly percentage of lanes opened, per month, at each of six selected crossings that process commercial vehicle traffic on the southwest border for the period fiscal years 2008 through 2012.[1] Figures 10 through 15 graphically depict the average hourly traffic volume and average hourly percentage of lanes open per month for each of the six selected crossings.

Table 8: Descriptions of Six Selected Crossings including Year Built and Renovated, and the Number of Available Commercial Lanes, Fiscal Years 2008 through 2012

Crossing name	Year built/last renovation	Number of lanes available
Otay Mesa: San Diego, California	1984/2009	• 10 commercial lanes available from October 1, 2007, to September 30, 2012
Mariposa: Nogales, Arizona	1976/2014[a]	• 4 commercial lanes available from October 1, 2007, to April 29, 2012 • 8 commercial lanes available from April 30, 2012, to September 30, 2012
Bridge of the Americas: El Paso, Texas	1967/2003	• 6 commercial lanes available from October 1, 2007, to September 30, 2012
Ysleta: El Paso, Texas	1991/2009	• 6 commercial lanes available from October 1, 2007, to October 20, 2008 • 8 commercial lanes available from October 21, 2008, to September 30, 2012
Columbia Solidarity: Laredo, Texas	1991/NA	• 8 commercial lanes available from October 1, 2007, to September 30, 2012
World Trade Bridge: Laredo, Texas	2000/2011	• 8 commercial lanes available from October 1, 2007, to April 14, 2011 • 15 commercial lanes available from April 15, 2011, to September 30, 2012

Source: GAO analysis of CBP data.

[1]We selected these six crossings based on their commercial traffic volume, geographic diversity, and representation of a mix of recent or ongoing infrastructure modernization projects.

[a]Mariposa is currently undergoing renovation. CBP officials report that these renovations are expected to be complete in fiscal year 2014.

Figure 4: The Otay Mesa Crossing near San Diego, California

Source: CBP.

Figure 5: Commercial Vehicle Primary Inspection Lanes at the Mariposa Crossing in Nogales, Arizona

Source: CBP.

Figure 6: The Bridge of the Americas Crossing in El Paso, Texas

Source: CBP.

Figure 7: The Ysleta Crossing in El Paso, Texas

Source: CBP

Figure 8: The Columbia Solidarity Bridge Crossing in Laredo, Texas

Source: CBP.

Figure 9: The World Trade Bridge Crossing in Laredo, Texas

Source: CBP.

Table 9: Average Hourly Traffic Volume and Average Hourly Percentage of Lanes Open Per Month at Otay Mesa Crossing near San Diego, California, Fiscal Years 2008 through 2012

Month and year	Average hourly traffic volume per month	Average hourly lane utilization per month (in percent)
October 2007	227	70
November 2007	229	83
December 2007	209	80
January 2008	190	83
February 2008	214	86
March 2008	229	83
April 2008	237	77
May 2008	246	74
June 2008	241	72
July, 2008	242	76
August 2008	233	73
September 2008	234	71
October 2008	229	71
November 2008	194	76
December 2008	178	80
January 2009	165	71
February 2009	168	67
March 2009	171	67
April 2009	187	72
May 2009	191	79
June,2009	202	80
July 2009	197	79
August 2009	197	78
September 2009	209	81
October 2009	221	81
November 2009	214	84
December 2009	194	83
January 2010	174	77
February 2010	195	80
March 2010	213	84
April 2010	219	84
May 2010	217	82
June 2010	223	85

Month and year	Average hourly traffic volume per month	Average hourly lane utilization per month (in percent)
July 2010	213	83
August 2010	212	82
September 2010	219	83
October 2010	215	81
November 2010	220	79
December 2010	188	80
January 2011	185	78
February 2011	202	83
March 2011	210	85
April 2011	212	84
May 2011	208	86
June 2011	227	89
July 2011	216	88
August 2011	216	88
September 2011	220	86
October 2011	226	86
November 2011	224	83
December 2011	189	85
January 2012	197	85
February 2012	206	83
March 2012	224	84
April 2012	223	82
May 2012	234	85
June 2012	232	88
July 2012	223	88
August 2012	230	89
September 2012	230	89

Source: GAO analysis of CBP data.

Table 10: Average Hourly Traffic Volume and Average Hourly Percentage of Lanes Open Per Month at Mariposa Crossing in Nogales, Arizona, Fiscal Years 2008 through 2012

Month and year	Average hourly traffic volume per month	Average hourly lane utilization per month (in percent)
October 2007	87	45
November 2007	114	64
December 2007	123	71
January 2008	137	71
February 2008	146	71
March 2008	150	70
April 2008	156	77
May 2008	166	94
June 2008	128	95
July 2008	102	46
August 2008	102	40
September 2008	96	39
October 2008	119	48
November 2008	127	56
December 2008	123	59
January 2009	137	73
February 2009	133	67
March 2009	132	63
April 2009	136	63
May 2009	131	70
June 2009	128	66
July 2009	91	55
August 2009	89	49
September 2009	93	46
October 2009	119	52
November 2009	127	60
December 2009	131	73
January 2010	151	80
February 2010	157	78
March 2010	161	80
April 2010	166	90
May 2010	174	90
June 2010	146	95

Month and year	Average hourly traffic volume per month	Average hourly lane utilization per month (in percent)
July 2010	102	87
August 2010	101	63
September 2010	100	65
October 2010	118	66
November 2010	135	78
December 2010	138	84
January 2011	150	89
February 2011	138	83
March 2011	134	71
April 2011	145	76
May 2011	168	92
June 2011	139	82
July 2011	103	57
August, 2011	103	57
September 2011	104	55
October 2011	122	61
November 2011	134	79
December 2011	127	72
January 2012	147	80
February 2012	151	84
March 2012	155	84
April 2012	159	83
May 2012	178	47
June 2012	142	48
July 2012	101	44
August 2012	103	41
September 2012	104	42

Source: GAO analysis of CBP data.

Table 11: Average Hourly Traffic Volume and Average Hourly Percentage of Lanes Open Per Month at Bridge of the Americas Crossing in El Paso, Texas, Fiscal Years 2008 through 2012

Month and year	Average hourly traffic volume per month	Average hourly lane utilization per month (in percent)
October 2007	164	87
November 2007	164	84
December 2007	143	91

Month and year	Average hourly traffic volume per month	Average hourly lane utilization per month (in percent)
January 2008	153	93
February 2008	164	93
March 2008	161	89
April 2008	168	94
May 2008	168	93
June 2008	175	93
July 2008	163	94
August 2008	168	89
September 2008	154	92
October 2008	154	91
November 2008	142	86
December 2008	120	83
January 2009	134	88
February 2009	132	77
March 2009	129	78
April 2009	118	75
May 2009	114	73
June 2009	117	76
July 2009	118	76
August 2009	122	77
September 2009	129	80
October 2009	129	81
November 2009	137	86
December 2009	122	82
January 2010	137	86
February 2010	144	91
March 2010	139	88
April 2010	140	90
May 2010	66	40
June 2010	126	70
July 2010	125	49
August 2010	129	48
September 2010	131	53
October 2010	130	63
November 2010	131	63
December 2010	111	63

Month and year	Average hourly traffic volume per month	Average hourly lane utilization per month (in percent)
January 2011	120	60
February 2011	117	65
March 2011	131	66
April 2011	132	68
May 2011	131	72
June 2011	133	72
July 2011	125	77
August 2011	132	81
September 2011	129	75
October 2011	127	71
November 2011	130	67
December 2011	109	49
January 2012	121	63
February 2012	118	54
March 2012	117	39
April 2012	117	52
May 2012	116	52
June 2012	116	74
July 2012	113	77
August 2012	114	79
September 2012	111	72

Source: GAO analysis of CBP data.

Table 12: Average Hourly Traffic Volume and Average Hourly Percentage of Lanes Open Per Month at Ysleta Crossing in El Paso, Texas, Fiscal Years 2008 through 2012

Month and year	Average hourly traffic volume per month	Average hourly lane utilization per month (in percent)
October 2007	131	92
November 2007	138	89
December 2007	119	90
January 2008	121	91
February 2008	135	94
March 2008	144	93
April 2008	137	94
May 2008	132	92
June 2008	138	95

Month and year	Average hourly traffic volume per month	Average hourly lane utilization per month (in percent)
July 2008	127	94
August 2008	131	88
September 2008	131	89
October 2008	131	81
November 2008	84	50
December 2008	71	45
January 2009	73	44
February 2009	73	41
March 2009	79	41
April, 2009	82	44
May 2009	83	46
June 2009	105	55
July 2009	102	54
August 2009	110	56
September 2009	118	58
October 2009	116	58
November 2009	115	58
December 2009	101	55
January 2010	103	55
February 2010	112	58
March 2010	117	57
April 2010	127	58
May 2010	179	77
June 2010	141	59
July 2010	121	33
August 2010	124	35
September 2010	130	37
October 2010	129	39
November 2010	130	38
December 2010	112	37
January 2011	120	36
February 2011	129	40
March 2011	140	40
April 2011	142	44
May 2011	131	43
June 2011	131	41

Month and year	Average hourly traffic volume per month	Average hourly lane utilization per month (in percent)
July 2011	122	42
August 2011	126	40
September 2011	130	41
October 2011	128	37
November 2011	123	35
December 2011	104	29
January 2012	123	38
February 2012	135	38
March 2012	135	27
April 2012	137	35
May 2012	141	35
June 2012	140	46
July 2012	127	44
August 2012	137	48
September 2012	139	46

Source: GAO analysis of CBP data.

Table 13: Average Hourly Traffic Volume and Average Hourly Percentage of Lanes Open Per Month at Columbia Solidarity Bridge Crossing in Laredo, Texas, Fiscal Years 2008 through 2012

Month and year	Average hourly traffic volume per month	Average hourly lane utilization per month (in percent)
October 2007	143	36
November 2007	138	36
December 2007	130	42
January 2008	133	45
February 2008	148	44
March 2008	143	46
April 2008	157	45
May 2008	145	45
June 2008	140	47
July 2008	123	45
August 2008	130	47
September 2008	122	46
October 2008	129	47
November 2008	122	45
December 2008	109	47

Month and year	Average hourly traffic volume per month	Average hourly lane utilization per month (in percent)
January 2009	105	46
February 2009	110	46
March 2009	102	41
April 2009	107	42
May 2009	96	43
June 2009	99	42
July 2009	96	39
August 2009	98	41
September 2009	108	39
October 2009	108	41
November 2009	114	40
December 2009	110	40
January 2010	119	38
February 2010	125	38
March 2010	134	36
April 2010	137	37
May 2010	126	38
June 2010	132	40
July 2010	115	38
August 2010	137	36
September 2010	132	36
October 2010	142	38
November 2010	146	39
December 2010	140	36
January 2011	138	37
February 2011	151	36
March 2011	155	36
April 2011	148	37
May 2011	139	36
June 2011	139	36
July 2011	130	37
August 2011	134	35
September 2011	144	36
October 2011	144	37
November 2011	145	36
December 2011	141	37

Month and year	Average hourly traffic volume per month	Average hourly lane utilization per month (in percent)
January 2012	142	37
February 2012	156	38
March 2012	158	37
April 2012	166	37
May 2012	151	37
June 2012	148	37
July 2012	141	37
August 2012	142	37
September 2012	140	36

Source: GAO analysis of CBP data.

Table 14: Average Hourly Traffic Volume and Average Hourly Percentage of Lanes Open Per Month at World Trade Bridge Crossing in Laredo, Texas, Fiscal Years 2008 through 2012

Month and year	Average hourly traffic volume per month	Average hourly lane utilization per month (in percent)
October 2007	327	87
November 2007	369	89
December 2007	349	90
January 2008	333	90
February 2008	363	89
March 2008	358	89
April 2008	373	90
May 2008	374	89
June 2008	374	90
July 2008	361	86
August 2008	367	89
September 2008	336	90
October 2008	361	93
November 2008	335	91
December 2008	306	91
January 2009	240	85
February 2009	247	83
March 2009	253	80
April 2009	255	73
May 2009	242	74
June 2009	307	80

Month and year	Average hourly traffic volume per month	Average hourly lane utilization per month (in percent)
July 2009	344	85
August 2009	369	84
September 2009	386	86
October 2009	384	85
November 2009	382	83
December 2009	386	84
January 2010	371	79
February 2010	397	77
March 2010	398	75
April 2010	418	79
May 2010	405	77
June 2010	414	79
July 2010	372	79
August 2010	418	78
September 2010	412	78
October 2010	405	79
November 2010	403	77
December 2010	391	77
January 2011	396	78
February 2011	419	76
March 2011	431	79
April 2011	443	71
May 2011	435	53
June 2011	432	51
July 2011	414	49
August 2011	431	52
September 2011	440	52
October 2011	435	48
November 2011	429	51
December 2011	403	50
January 2012	421	49
February 2012	470	54
March 2012	490	55
April 2012	480	57
May 2012	486	58
June 2012	488	57

Month and year	Average hourly traffic volume per month	Average hourly lane utilization per month (in percent)
July 2012	462	55
August 2012	481	55
September 2012	462	54

Source: GAO analysis of CBP data.

Figure 10: Average Hourly Traffic Volume and Average Hourly Percentage of Lanes Open Per Month at Otay Mesa Crossing near San Diego, California, Fiscal Year 2008 through 2012

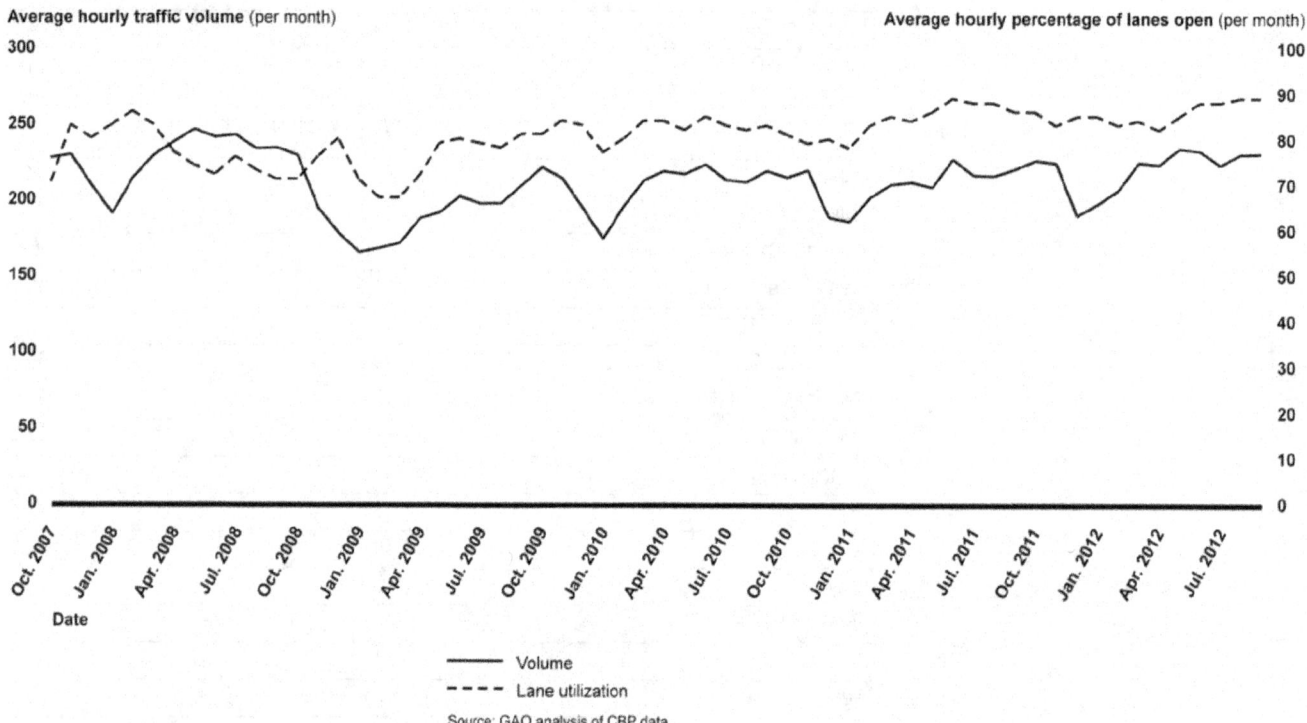

Source: GAO analysis of CBP data.

Figure 11: Average Hourly Traffic Volume and Average Hourly Percentage of Lanes Open Per Month at the Mariposa Crossing in Nogales, Arizona, Fiscal Year 2008 through 2012

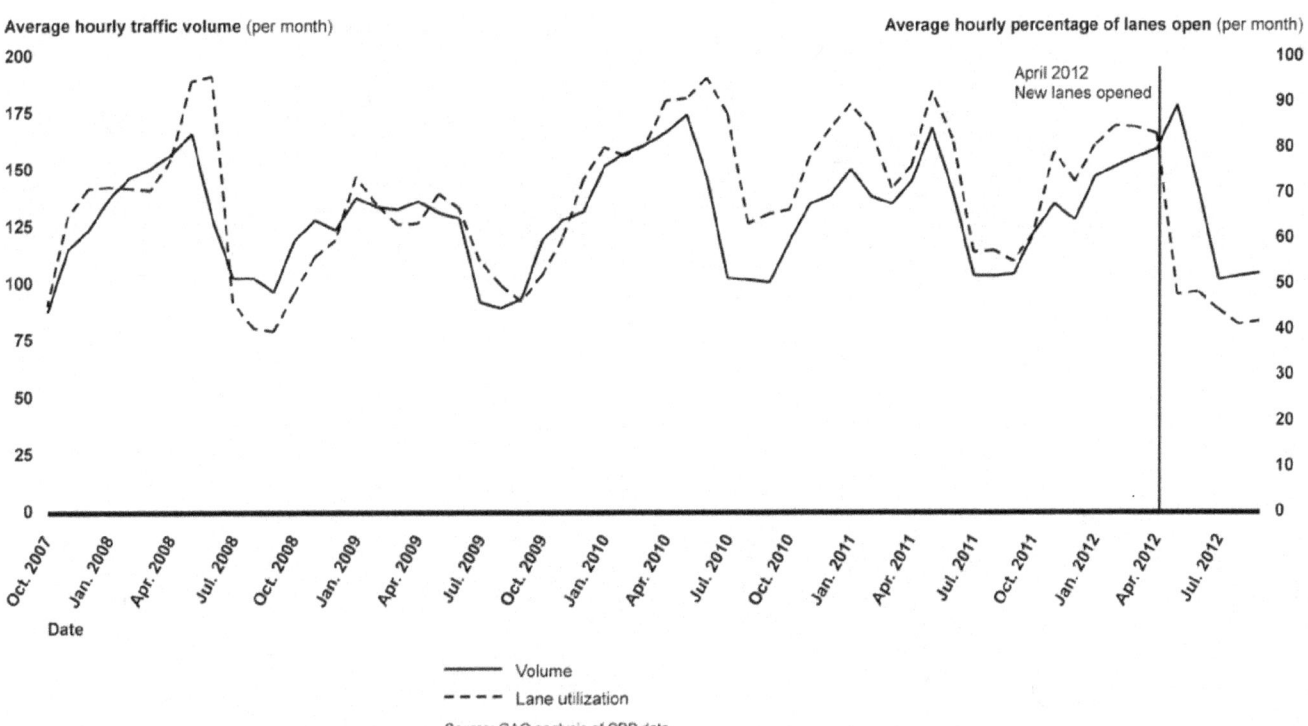

Source: GAO analysis of CBP data.

Figure 12: Average Hourly Traffic Volume and Average Hourly Percentage of Lanes Open Per Month at the Bridge of the Americas Crossing in El Paso, Texas, Fiscal Year 2008 through 2012

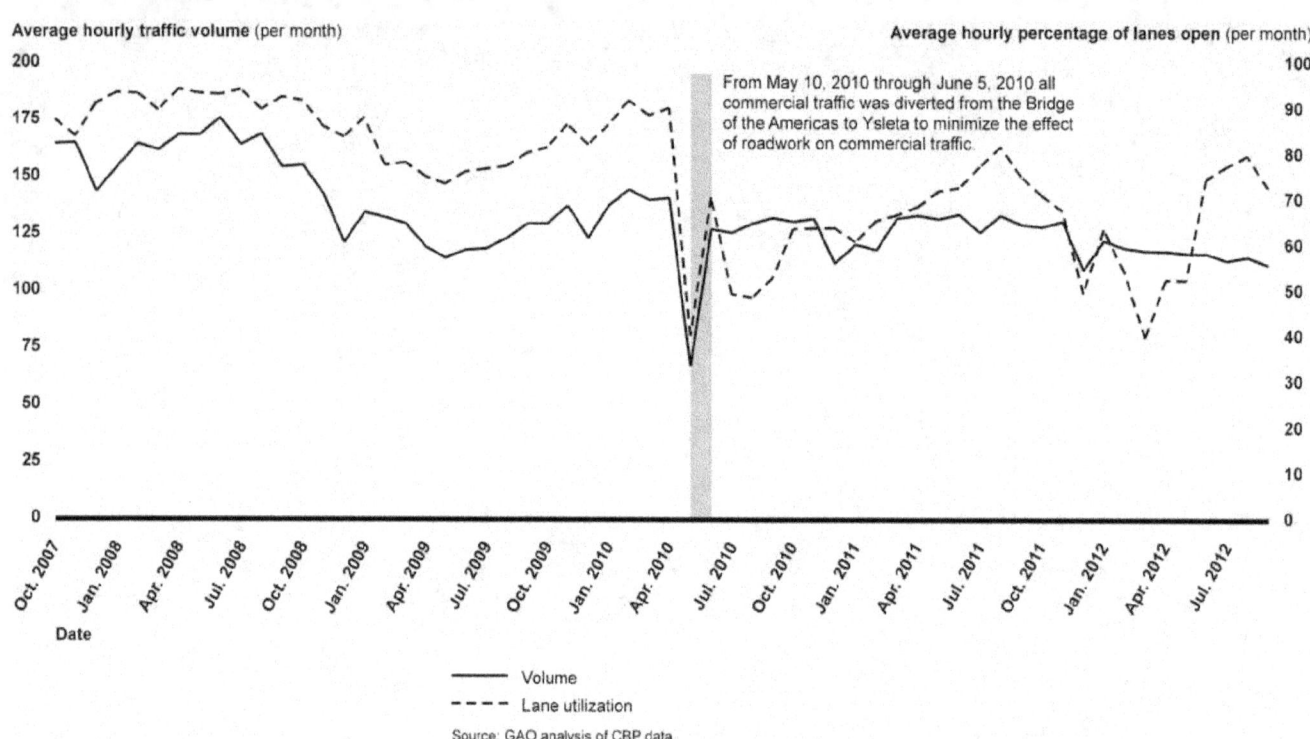

Source: GAO analysis of CBP data.

Figure 13: Average Hourly Traffic Volume and Average Hourly Percentage of Lanes Open Per Month at Ysleta Crossing in El Paso, Texas, Fiscal Year 2008 through 2012

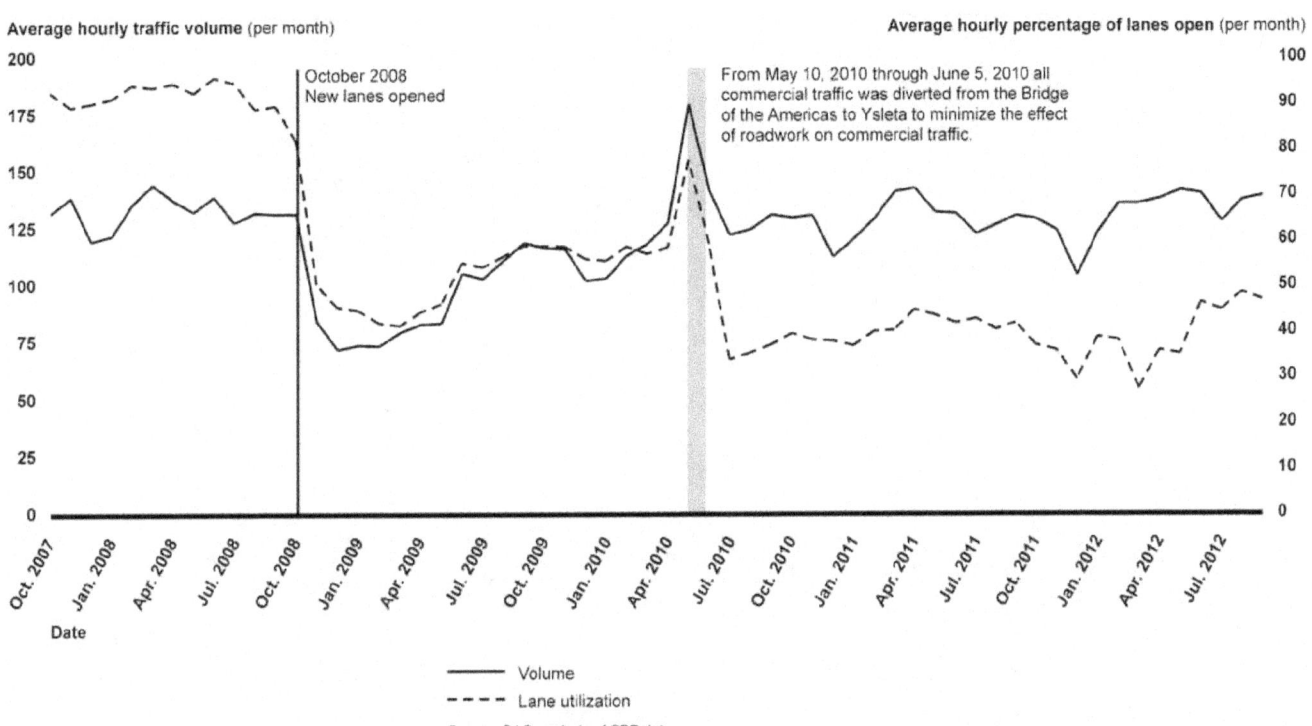

Source: GAO analysis of CBP data.

Figure 14: Average Hourly Traffic Volume and Average Hourly Percentage of Lanes Open Per Month at Columbia Solidarity Bridge Crossing in Laredo, Texas, Fiscal Year 2008 through 2012

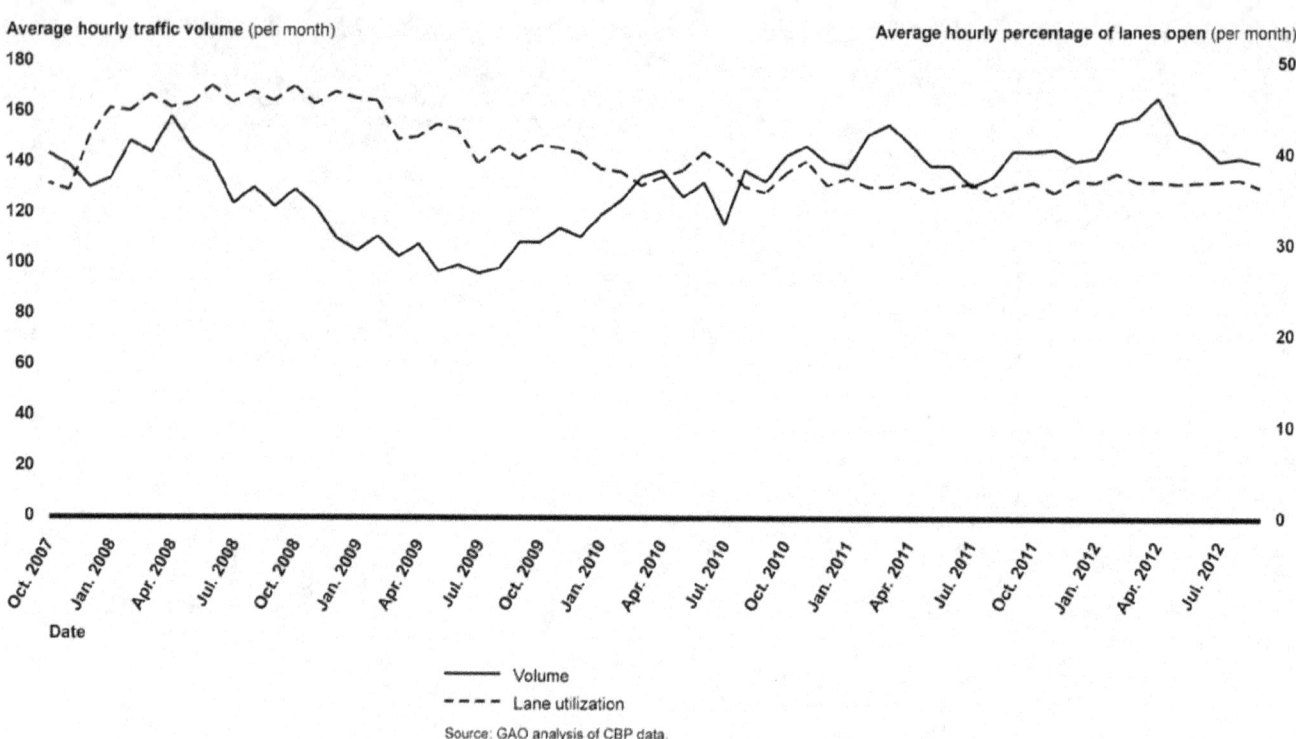

Source: GAO analysis of CBP data.

Figure 15: Average Hourly Traffic Volume and Average Hourly Percentage of Lanes Open Per Month at World Trade Bridge Crossing in Laredo, Texas, Fiscal Year 2008 through 2012

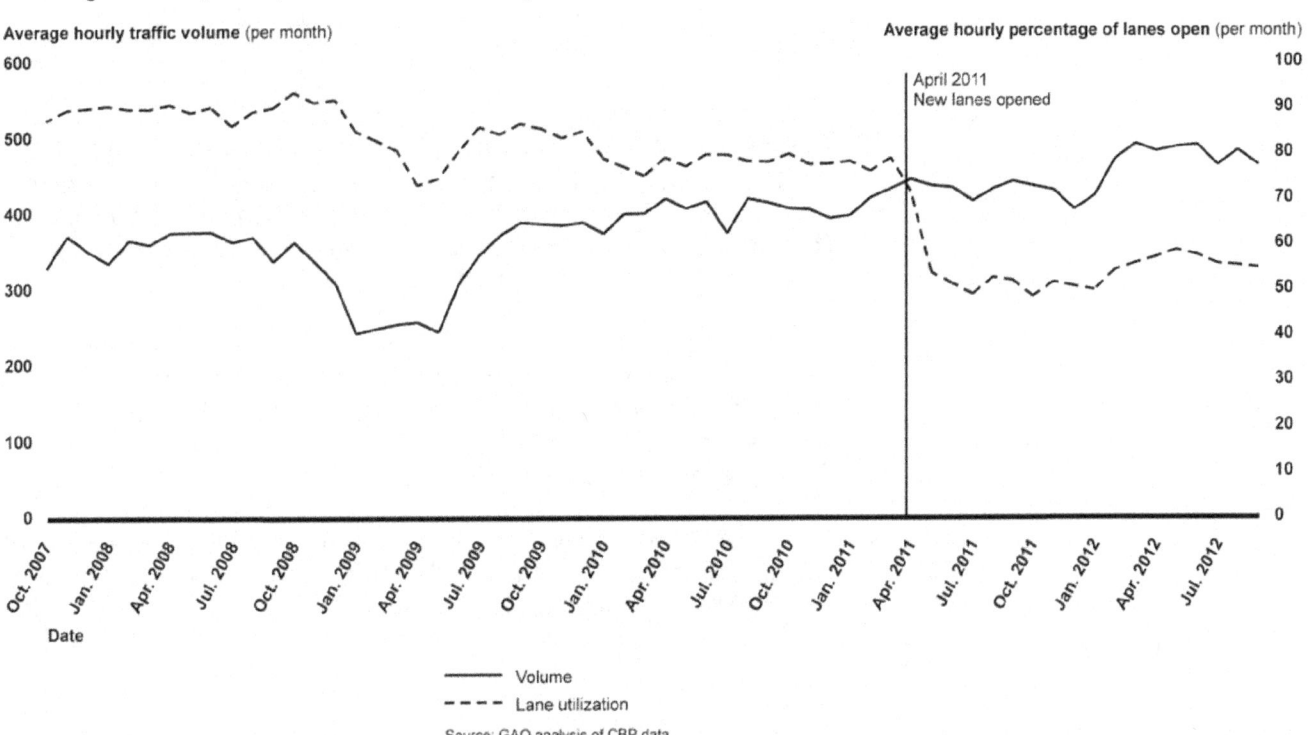

Source: GAO analysis of CBP data.

Appendix VI: Performance Measures for U.S. Customs and Border Protection Activities, Fiscal Year 2013

Table 15 lists the 28 performance measures DHS and CBP are using in fiscal year 2013 to assess and report on CBP progress toward the agency's security and trade facilitation goals. These CBP-focused performance measures include the following:

- Nine measures selected by DHS as Government Performance and Results Act (GPRA) measures.[1] (These are also called strategic measures within the department.) These measures are aligned with the goals and objectives in DHS's *Quadrennial Homeland Security Review Report* and publicly reported to communicate achievement of these strategic goals and objectives.[2]

- Fifteen management measures that are not reported publicly but rather inform internal CBP decisions on program priorities and resource allocation, and to monitor progress and performance. CBP officials report, for example, that these measures are used in crafting the department's budget justification.

- Four CBP Office of Field Operations (OFO) operational measures that capture former GPRA measures that OFO uses internally to evaluate senior officials' performance, for example.[3]

---

[1]In fiscal year 2013, DHS has designated 84 GPRA performance measures—9 of which focus on CBP efforts.

[2]The agency's security and trade facilitation goals are articulated in DHS's February 2010 *Quadrennial Homeland Security Review Report,* which outlined a strategic framework for homeland security. See DHS, *Quadrennial Homeland Security Review Report: A Strategic Framework for a Secure Homeland* (Washington, D.C.: February 2010).

[3]According to CBP officials, OFO is the only office within CBP that maintains such operational measures.

Table 15: U.S. Customs and Border Protection-Focused Performance Measures, Fiscal Year 2013

Type of performance measure		Performance measure name	Fiscal year 2013 target
Government Performance and Results Act / strategic performance measures	1	Number of apprehensions on the southwest border between the ports of entry	< 391,000
	2	Percent of people apprehended multiple times along the southwest border	18%
	3	Percent of detected conventional aircraft incursions resolved along all borders of the United States	100%
	4	Percent of cargo by value imported into the U.S. by participants in CBP trade partnership programs	57%
	5	Percent of import revenue successfully collected	100%
	6	Percent of imports compliant with U.S. trade laws	97.5%
	7	Amount of smuggled outbound currency seized at ports of entry	$30 million
	8	Number of smuggled outbound weapons seized at ports of entry	400
	9	Percent of inbound cargo identified by CBP as potentially high risk that is assessed or scanned prior to departure or at arrival at a U.S. port of entry	FOUO[a]
Management performance measures	1	Average number of apprehensions for persons with multiple apprehensions along the southwest border	2.48
	2	Number of joint operations conducted along the southwest border by Border Patrol agents and Mexican law enforcement partners	11
	3	Number of joint operations conducted along the northern border by Border Patrol agents and Canadian law enforcement partners	18
	4	Percent of apprehensions at Border Patrol checkpoints	< 5%
	5	Percent of air support launches accomplished to support Homeland Security missions	> 95%
	6	Percent of pharmaceutical, health, and chemical industry imports compliant with U.S. trade laws	98%
	7	Percent of petroleum industry imports compliant with U.S. trade laws	95%
	8	Value of shipments seized as a result of intellectual property rights violations	$136 million
	9	Number of shipments seized as a result of intellectual property rights violations	24,000
	10	Compliance rate for Customs-Trade Partnership Against Terrorism (C-TPAT) members with established C-TPAT security criteria[b]	94%
	11	Percent of land border passengers compliant with laws, rules, and regulations	99.5%
	12	Percent of air passengers compliant with laws, rules, and regulations	98%
	13	Percent of border vehicle passengers in compliance with agricultural quarantine regulations	95.5%
	14	Percent of international air passengers in compliance with agricultural quarantine regulations	95.5%
	15	Percent of time TECS is available to end users[c]	99%

Type of performance measure		Performance measure name	Fiscal year 2013 target
Office of Field Operations' operational performance measures[d]	1	Percent increase in travelers to the U.S. enrolled in a Trusted Traveler program (cumulative)	16%
	2	Percent of individuals screened against law enforcement databases for entry into the United States	FOUO[a]
	3	Air passenger interdiction rate for major violations	FOUO[a]
	4	Land border interdiction rate for major violations	FOUO[a]

Source: GAO analysis of CBP performance measurement documents.

[a]The specific performance target is designated by CBP as for official use only (FOUO).

[b]C-TPAT is a customs-to-business partnership program that provides benefits to supply chain companies that agree to comply with predetermined security measures

[c]TECS is the principal system used by CBP officers at the border to assist with screening and determinations regarding admiss bility of arriving persons.

[d]According to CBP officials, OFO is the only office within CBP that maintains such operational measures.

Appendix VII: Comments from the Department of Homeland Security

U.S. Department of Homeland Security
Washington, DC 20528

July 5, 2013

Rebecca Gambler
Director, Homeland Security and Justice Issues
U.S. Government Accountability Office
441 G Street, NW
Washington, DC 20548

Re: Draft Report GAO-13-603, "U.S.–MEXICO BORDER: CBP Action Needed to Improve Wait
Time Data and Measure Outcomes of Trade Facilitation Efforts"

Dear Ms. Gambler:

Thank you for the opportunity to review and comment on this draft report. The U.S. Department of
Homeland Security (DHS) appreciates the U.S. Government Accountability Office's (GAO's) work
in planning and conducting its review and issuing this report.

As the report highlights, trade between Mexico and the United States is important to U.S.
economic health, and the number of commercial vehicles carrying goods across the U.S.–Mexico
border is on the rise. U.S. Customs and Border Protection (CBP) recognizes that the length of
time commercial vehicles wait in line at the border affects trade activity between the United
States and Mexico. CBP is taking action to develop a high-level trade facilitation goal to support
a strong economy by expediting legitimate trade.

The draft report contained four recommendations with which the Department concurs.
Specifically, GAO recommended that the Commissioner of CBP:

Recommendation 1: Identify and carry-out steps that can be taken to help CBP port officials
overcome challenges to consistent implementation of existing wait time estimation
methodologies. Steps for ensuring consistent implementation of these methodologies could
include, for example, implementing the fiscal year 2008 WHTI report recommendations to use
closed-circuit television cameras to measure wait time in real time and provide a standardized
measurement and validation tool.

Response: Concur. CBP's Office of Field Operations (OFO) will continue to work
cooperatively with the bi-national Border Wait Time work group (Canada Border Security
Agency, Transport Canada, and Federal Highway Administration [FHWA]) and regional
transportation stakeholders to leverage existing technologies (such as radio frequency
identification, inductive loops, Bluetooth, etc.) and to identify emerging technologies for
automating the measurement of vehicle wait times at the land border.

The resulting automated land border wait time management solution will enable CBP/OFO to:

1) eliminate manual reporting of wait times;

2) obtain standard, reliable, and consistent wait time and delay information in real time;

3) improve customer service by increasing availability of staff for enforcement operations;

4) improve agency transparency by enabling land border wait times to be easily shared with participating agencies and regional traffic management centers;

5) reduce delays in freight movement and loss of business income at the regional, state, and national level; and

6) reduce environmental costs by decreasing pollution and carbon emissions associated with heavy congestion.

If funding is available, CBP/OFO has a goal to automate the estimation and reporting of border wait times. CBP/OFO has researched available and emerging wait time methodologies, conducted pilots in automated wait time measurement, and met with various stakeholders as they have begun to conduct separate pilots.

CBP/OFO will work proactively to validate the accuracy and usefulness of the wait time estimates produced by these solutions. If credible, CBP/OFO will adopt these estimates for use in its Border Wait Time (BWT) Web site; replacing existing manual estimates and processes. CBP has already developed (in concert with FHWA) a data schema for accepting external wait time estimates into the BWT site. The BWT site is currently used to report border crossing wait time estimates to trade, stakeholders, and the traveling public. Corrective actions toward meeting this recommendation include: establishing the internal/external stakeholder group; and identifying the best candidate technologies to pilot. Estimated Completion Date (ECD): June 30, 2014.

Recommendation 2: In consultation with FHWA and state DOTs, assess the feasibility of replacing current methods of manually calculating wait times with automated methods, which could include assessing all of the associated costs and benefits, options for how the agency will use and publicly report the results of automated data collection, the potential trade-offs associated with moving to this new system, and other factors such as those influencing the possible expansion of existing automation efforts to the 34 other locations that currently report wait times but have no automation projects under way.

Response: Concur. Various wait time measurement technologies are currently in production in the Cascade Corridor, Niagara Region, and at several crossings on the southern border. These solutions continue to mature and show great promise for measuring vehicle wait times that can be used by border agencies to manage delays. It should be noted that calculating vehicle wait times, at the surface, appears to be a simple process; however, in reality, calibrating an effective,

2

reliable, and accurate measurement system is a complicated endeavor with many variables encompassing local, regional, and international stakeholders.

CBP has consulted with FHWA and multiple state Departments of Transportation (DOTs) to assess automated wait time feasibility. Further, CBP has conducted a pilot automated wait time solution in concert with FHWA and other stakeholders. Whereas the pilot did not yield a truly effective automated solution, it did improve upon wait time estimates when compared to manual estimation; and CBP successfully integrated the solution's data into its BWT Web site. CBP has also consulted with several of its DHS Centers of Excellence, most notably the BORDERs Center of Excellence (University of Arizona). Emerging and refined technologies, in conjunction with lessons learned during the pilot, indicate that from a technology standpoint automating wait time estimation is extremely feasible. Feasibility is reduced from a financing, funding, and operating standpoint. We request that this recommendation be considered resolved and closed.

Recommendation 3: Document the methodology and process OFO uses to allocate staff to land ports of entry on the southwest border, including the rationales and factors considered in making these decisions.

Response: Concur. CBP/OFO will develop a standardized process for allocating CBP Officers that uses Workload Staffing Model results; current and future operational priorities and threats; and historical staffing levels and patterns. The process will document both phases of the allocation:

1) allocations to each field office, and

2) further allocation down to the port level.

The process also will document assumptions, factors and concerns to be used at all levels to guide the decision-making and allocation process. ECD: December 31, 2013.

Recommendation 4: Develop outcome-oriented performance measures or proxy measures to capture the impact of CBP's trade facilitation efforts, such as measures to determine the extent to which CBP trusted shipper programs have met their goals.

Response: Concur. CBP/OFO recognizes the need to maintain a strong economy by expediting legitimate trade and understands that meeting its high-level trade facilitation goal is critical to making this happen. Although past CBP measurement efforts have focused largely on the more immediate concerns of security, enforcement, and compliance; OFO concurs with the importance of outcome-based measurement in support of CBP's trade facilitation efforts. CBP is currently engaged in two studies that address both the security and facilitation aspects of trade. The first is the DHS QHSR Trade Flows Study. The second is the National Security Staff Trans-border Directorate's Trusted Trader efforts in support of the National Strategy for Global Supply Chain Security. Participating in these high-level initiatives within the Department and the Administration will help provide additional clarity in defining the specific goals going forward for trusted trader programs.

3

OFO will create a team of subject matter experts from OFO trade-related programs to identify several outcome measures and/or acceptable proxy measures for trade facilitation. OFO will also collaborate with private-sector entities such as the Commercial Operations Advisory Council in order to identify metrics of greatest concern. OFO will work towards putting into place at least two new trade facilitation outcome measures and/or proxy measures as OFO operational measures, following the general guidance outlined in this report. ECD: June 30, 2014.

Again, thank you for the opportunity to review and provide comments on this draft report. Technical comments were previously provided under separate cover. Please feel free to contact me if you have any questions. We look forward to working with you in the future.

Sincerely,

Jim H. Crumpacker
Director
Departmental GAO-OIG Liaison Office

4

Appendix VIII: GAO Contact and Staff Acknowledgments

GAO Contact	Rebecca Gambler, (202) 512-8777 or GamblerR@gao.gov
Staff Acknowledgments	In addition to the contact named above, Lacinda Ayers, Assistant Director; Claudia Becker; Sarah Kaczmarek; and Michael Lenington made key contributions to this report. Also contributing to this report were Pedro Almoguera, Frances Cook, Juan Gobel, Eric Hauswirth, Phil Herr, Stan Kostyla, Jessica Orr, Minette Richardson, and Loren Yager.

GAO's Mission	The Government Accountability Office, the audit, evaluation, and investigative arm of Congress, exists to support Congress in meeting its constitutional responsibilities and to help improve the performance and accountability of the federal government for the American people. GAO examines the use of public funds; evaluates federal programs and policies; and provides analyses, recommendations, and other assistance to help Congress make informed oversight, policy, and funding decisions. GAO's commitment to good government is reflected in its core values of accountability, integrity, and reliability.
Obtaining Copies of GAO Reports and Testimony	The fastest and easiest way to obtain copies of GAO documents at no cost is through GAO's website (http://www.gao.gov). Each weekday afternoon, GAO posts on its website newly released reports, testimony, and correspondence. To have GAO e-mail you a list of newly posted products, go to http://www.gao.gov and select "E-mail Updates."
Order by Phone	The price of each GAO publication reflects GAO's actual cost of production and distribution and depends on the number of pages in the publication and whether the publication is printed in color or black and white. Pricing and ordering information is posted on GAO's website, http://www.gao.gov/ordering.htm. Place orders by calling (202) 512-6000, toll free (866) 801-7077, or TDD (202) 512-2537. Orders may be paid for using American Express, Discover Card, MasterCard, Visa, check, or money order. Call for additional information.
Connect with GAO	Connect with GAO on Facebook, Flickr, Twitter, and YouTube. Subscribe to our RSS Feeds or E-mail Updates. Listen to our Podcasts. Visit GAO on the web at www.gao.gov.
To Report Fraud, Waste, and Abuse in Federal Programs	Contact: Website: http://www.gao.gov/fraudnet/fraudnet.htm E-mail: fraudnet@gao.gov Automated answering system: (800) 424-5454 or (202) 512-7470
Congressional Relations	Katherine Siggerud, Managing Director, siggerudk@gao.gov, (202) 512-4400, U.S. Government Accountability Office, 441 G Street NW, Room 7125, Washington, DC 20548
Public Affairs	Chuck Young, Managing Director, youngc1@gao.gov, (202) 512-4800 U.S. Government Accountability Office, 441 G Street NW, Room 7149 Washington, DC 20548

Please Print on Recycled Paper.

www.ingramcontent.com/pod-product-compliance
Lightning Source LLC
Chambersburg PA
CBHW080312290526
45790CB00005B/2009